The Big Book of Fables

THE · BIG · BOOK · OF
·FABLES·

EDITED·BY·WALTER·JERROLD·
·AND·ILLUSTRATED·BY·
·CHARLES·ROBINSON·

·AND·

JANE HARVEY

PORTLAND HOUSE
NEW YORK

This edition published 1987 by Portland House
Distributed by Crown Publishers, Inc.
225 Park Avenue South
New York, New York 10003

This edition. Copyright © Lamboll House, 1987
Black and White illustrations.
Copyright © The Estate of Charles Robinson, 1987
Color illustrations. Copyright © Lamboll House, 1987

ISBN 0-517-63790-1

Printed and bound in Hungary
h g f e d c b a

DEDICATION

To
Alan

·INTRODUCTION·

S fables—stories in which birds and beasts, trees and insects, speak in the manner of men—belong to the oldest kind of tales that are told, to the kind in which savage as well as civilized peoples have alike delighted, so in a sense they may be said to belong to the newest, for each of us begins the lessons of life as they are presented in these shortest of short stories. Even the very youngest reader of this book will probably already know something of one or two of the stories, for some of them have become so familiar to everybody, that references to them are part of everyday talk. A small child who has refused to let another have a toy with which he was not playing may well wonder why his nurse or mother has called him "a little dog-in-the-manger"—in one of these stories he will learn why, and will surely do his best not to deserve the name again! That is the first use of the fable, as we now understand it—to teach us how to behave to others. But it does not teach us by merely saying "be good", "be kind", "be just"; it teaches us by telling a delightful little story with a "moral". The story is for our amusement, and the moral is one of the little lessons which we may learn from it.

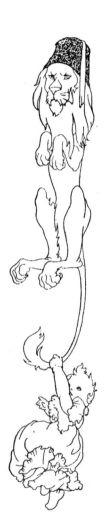

We may well laugh, for instance, at that other foolish dog that dropped his piece of meat into the water while greedily trying to snatch the reflection which he thought another piece of meat, but having done so we are likely to remember that greediness is a foolish thing which soon brings about its own punishment. There are some people who pretend to dislike these morals, but they are short-sighted folks who think that a thing should be only beautiful, and do not see that it is still more beautiful if it is useful as well. Fortunately most people do not agree with those short-sighted folks, and thus it is that some of our fables have been repeated again and again, not only for hundreds, but actually for thousands of years.

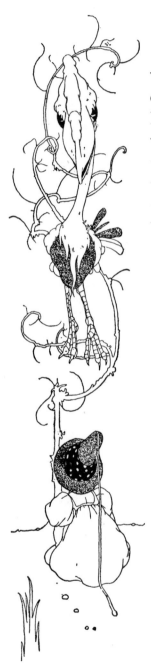

Yes, even thousands of years; for the man whose name is most commonly associated with our fables is that of Æsop, who died nearly two thousand five hundred years ago. It is true that we do not know much about Æsop; it is probable that most of the stories to which his name is attached were never told by him, and it may certainly be said that he did not invent the fable; yet he is of interest as being the first author whose name is associated with these little stories. Æsop is said to have been a Greek slave who was born about six hundred and twenty years before the birth of Christ, and died at about the age of sixty. Some accounts describe him as having been deformed; but these accounts, it must be remembered, were written long after his death, and it is not really known what he was like. Some of the stories of him say that though at one time a slave, he was given his freedom by his master and lived for a while at the court of King Crœsus, and that he once dined with those philosophers known as the Seven Sages. When the people of Athens were thinking of changing their ruler, Æsop is said to have told them his fable of "The Frogs Choose a King" for the purpose of pointing out to them how it was possible, in the eagerness to change, to pass from bad to worse. Æsop is indeed supposed to have told his stories always by word of mouth, for it is not known whether he ever wrote them down. It was seven or eight hundred years after his death that the first collection of the fables that we know as his was made by a writer named Babrius—supposed to have been a Roman living in the East.

Very little is indeed known with any certainty of any of the old writers or collectors of fables. The fables of Bidpai (or Pilpay) were early Oriental tales; but perhaps the most generally known name in association with fables after that of Æsop is that of Jean de la Fontaine, one of the leading French men of letters of his time. La Fontaine, who was born in 1621 and died in 1695, published his first *Fables* in 1668. Several of his stories are the same as those associated with the earlier collections — though he set them forth in a new verse form—and many of the verse fables given in this " Big Book " are translated from La Fontaine. Many later writers have given us fables, though few with the neat brevity of Æsop. Possibly a score of different authors, or even more, are represented in this volume. Here will be found one, *The Raven*, by

William Cowper, the author of *The Diverting History of John Gilpin*, and one, *The Mountain and the Squirrel*, by the great American author, Ralph Waldo Emerson, as well as some by yet more recent writers. In all, the intention is the same, to present a little story which shall entertain us by what it tells, and teach us by what it implies. As La Fontaine himself put it—

"We yawn at sermons, but we gladly turn
To moral tales, and so amused we learn".

WALTER JERROLD.

CONTENTS

CONTENTS

CONTENTS

CONTENTS

CONTENTS

CONTENTS

ILLUSTRATIONS

COLOURED PLATES

ILLUSTRATIONS

BLACK-AND-WHITE PLATES

ILLUSTRATIONS

ILLUSTRATIONS

ILLUSTRATIONS

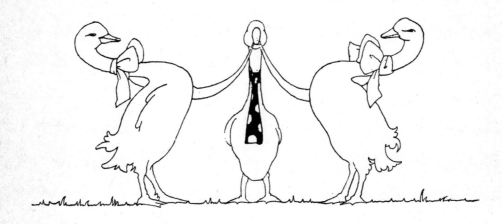

Here b;egi
nsthe b
ig bo"
ig bo"
ffab
les"
!

A Peacock and a Crane

As a peacock and a crane were in company together, the peacock spread his tail, and challenged the other to show him such a fan of feathers. The crane, upon this, sprang up into the air, and calls to the peacock to follow him if he could.

"You brag of your plumes," says he, "that are fair indeed to the eye, but no way useful or fit for any manner of service."

MORAL.—*That which is useful is of more importance than that which is merely ornamental.*

The Lion and the Hunter

A braggart, lover of the chase,
Had lost a dog of valued race,
And thought him in a lion's maw.
He ask'd a shepherd whom he saw:
"Pray show me, man, the robber's place,
And I'll have justice in the case."
    "'Tis on this mountainside,"
    The shepherd man replied.
"The tribute of a sheep I pay,
Each month, and where I please I stray."
    Out leap'd the lion as he spake,
        And came that way with agile feet.
    The braggart, prompt his flight to take,
        Cried: "Jove, Oh, grant a safe retreat!"

MORAL.—

A danger close at hand
    Of courage is the test.
It shows us who will stand—
    Whose legs will run their best.

"THE BRAGGART, PROMPT HIS FLIGHT TO TAKE"

Two Travellers and a Bag of Money

As two travellers were upon the way together, one of them stooped, and took up something.

"Look ye here," said he, "I've found a bag of money."

"No," said the other; "when two friends are together, you may not say *I* have found it, but *we* have found it."

The word was no sooner out, but immediately comes a hue and cry after a gang of thieves that had taken a purse upon the road.

"Lord, brother," says he that had the bag, "we shall be utterly undone!"

"Oh, fie!" says the other; "you must not say *we* shall be undone, but *I* shall be undone; for if I'm to have no part in the finding, sure I'll never go halves in the punishment."

MORAL.—*It is necessary to take the bad as well as the good of a bargain.*

TWO TRAVELLERS FIND A BAG OF MONEY

A Countryman and a Snake

A countryman happened in a hard winter to spy under a hedge a snake that was half-frozen to death. The man was good-natured and took it up, and kept it in his bosom till warmth brought it to life again; and so soon as ever it was in condition to do mischief it bit the very man that saved the life of it.

"Ah, thou ungrateful wretch!" says he; "is that venomous ill-nature of thine to be satisfied with nothing less than the ruin of thy preserver?"

MORAL.—*Discrimination should be used even in benefactions.*

THE COUNTRYMAN FINDS A SNAKE

7

𝕬 𝕳untsman and a 𝕮urrier

A currier bought a bearskin of a huntsman, and paid him ready money for it. The huntsman told him that he would kill a bear next day, and he should have the skin. The currier, for his curiosity, went out with the huntsman to the chase, and mounted a tree, whence he might see the sport. The huntsman advanced very bravely up to the den where the bear lay, and sent in the dogs upon him. The bear rushed out immediately, and, the man missing his aim, the bear overturned him. So the fellow held his breath, and lay stone still, as if he were dead. The bear snuffed and smelt him, took him for a carcass, and so left him. When the bear was gone, and the danger over, down came the currier from the tree, and bade the huntsman rise.

"Hark ye, my friend," says the currier, "the bear whispered somewhat in your ear. What was it, I prithee?"

"Oh," says the huntsman, "he bade me have a care, for the future, to make sure of the bear, before I sell his skin!"

MORAL.—*It is not good for a man to undertake more than he can fulfil.*

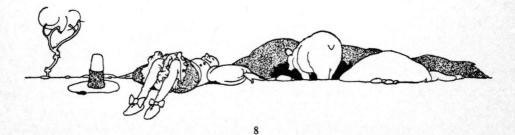

A Peacock and a Crane

The Hornets and the Bees

"AND MOUNTED A TREE"

𝔄 𝔥𝔢𝔫 𝔞𝔫𝔡 𝔊𝔬𝔩𝔡𝔢𝔫 𝔈𝔤𝔤𝔰

A certain good woman had a hen that laid her golden eggs, and so she thought that the bird must have a gold mine in it. Upon this presumption she cut it up to search for hidden treasure; but upon the dissection found her just like other hens, and that the  hope of getting more had betrayed her to the loss of that which she had possessed.

MORAL.—*To be content may be rich, while covetousness may bring a man to beggary.*

"SHE CUT IT UP TO SEARCH FOR TREASURE"

The Hornets and the Bees

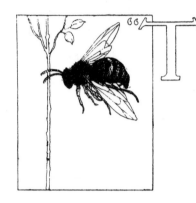

"THE artist by his work is known."
A piece of honeycomb, one day,
Discover'd as a waif and stray,
The hornets treated as their own.
Their title did the bees dispute,
And brought before a wasp the
  suit.
The judge was puzzled to decide,
For nothing could be testified
Save that around this honeycomb
There had been seen, as if at home,
Some longish, brownish, buzzing creatures,
Much like the bees in wings and features.
But what of that? for marks the same
The hornets, too, could truly claim.
Between assertion and denial,
The wasp, in doubt, proclaim'd new trial;
And, hearing what an anthill swore,
Could see no clearer than before.
"What use, I pray, of this expense?"
At last exclaim'd a bee of sense.
  "We've labour'd months in this affair,
  And now are only where we were.
  Meanwhile the honey runs to waste:
'T is time the judge should show some haste.
The parties, sure, have had sufficient bleeding,
Without more fuss of scrawls and pleading.

"AND BROUGHT BEFORE A WASP THE SUIT"

THE HORNETS AND THE BEES

Let's set ourselves to work, these drones and we,
And then all eyes the truth may plainly see,
 Whose art it is that can produce
 The magic cells, the nectar juice."
  The hornets, flinching on their part,
  Show that the work transcends their art.
  The wasp at length their title sees,
  And gives the honey to the bees.

Moral.—

Would that all suits at laws with us
 Might each be managed thus:
That we might, in the Turkish mode,
Have simple common sense for code!
They then were short and cheap affairs,
Instead of stretching on like ditches,
Ingulfing in their course all riches,
The parties leaving for their shares
The shells (and shells their might be moister)
From which the court had suck'd the oyster.

The Wolf accusing the Fox before the Monkey

A wolf, affirming his belief
That he had suffer'd by a thief,
  Brought up his neighbour fox—
Of whom it was by all confess'd,
His character was not the best—
  To fill the prisoner's box.
As judge between these vermin,
A monkey graced the ermine;
And truly other gifts of Themis
  Did scarcely seem his;
For while each party pled his cause,
Appealing boldly to the laws,
And much the question vex'd,
Our monkey sat perplex'd.

Their words and wrath expended,
Their strife at length was ended;
When, by their malice taught,
The judge this judgment brought:
"Your characters, my friends, I long have known,
 As on this trial clearly shown;
And hence I fine you both—the grounds at large
 To state would little profit—
You, wolf, in short, as bringing groundless charge,
 You, fox, as guilty of it."

Come at it right or wrong, the judge opined
No other than a villain could be fined.

MORAL.—*A man should be sure of his own innocence before
accusing another.*

𝕬 𝕱𝖑𝖞 𝖚𝖕𝖔𝖓 𝖙𝖍𝖊 𝖂𝖍𝖊𝖊𝖑

"What a dust I do raise!" says the fly upon the coach wheel. "And what a rate I do drive at," says the same fly again, upon the horse's back.

MORAL.—*It is very easy to exaggerate our own importance.*

"A BEE PRICKED HIS FINGER"

Love Stung by a Bee

As Cupid was amusing himself among the flowers and the roses, a bee pricked his finger, and away goes he with a lamentable story to his mother of a serpent that had stung him.

"Alas for thee, poor simple wretch," cries the mother, "to make such a business of a pricked finger, and at the same time to be so insensible of the anguish of so many wounded hearts!"

MORAL.—*None are so unmerciful to other people as those that are the most indulgent to themselves.*

𝔄 Countryman and a River

A countryman that was to pass a river, sounded it up and down to try where it was most fordable, and upon trial he made this observation on it: where the water ran smooth he found it deepest, and, on the contrary, shallowest where it made most noise.

MORAL.—*A silent enemy is more dangerous than one who babbles much.*

"SHALLOWEST WHERE IT MADE MOST NOISE"

𝕬 𝔚𝔬𝔩𝔣 𝔞𝔫𝔡 𝔞 𝕮𝔯𝔞𝔫𝔢

A wolf had got a bone in his throat, and could think of no better instrument to ease him of it than the bill of a crane; so he went and treated with a crane to help him out with it, upon condition of a very considerable reward for his pains. The crane did him the good office, and then claimed his promise.

"Why, how now, Impudence!" says the other; "do you put your head into the mouth of a wolf, and then, when you've brought it out again safe and sound, do you talk of a reward? Why, sirrah, you have your head again, and is not that a sufficient recompense?"

MORAL.—*He that has to deal with a villain may be glad to escape with his skin.*

"THE CRANE DID HIM THE GOOD OFFICE"

THE TWO POTS

The Hare and the Tortoise

A Dog and a Cock upon a Journey

The Two Pots

HERE were two pots that stood near one another by the side of a river, the one of brass and the other of clay. The water overflowed the banks and carried them both away. The earthen vessel kept aloof from the other as much as possible.

"Fear nothing," says the brass pot; "I'll do you no hurt."

"No, no," says the other, "not willingly; but if we should happen to knock by chance, it would be the same thing to me, so that you and I shall never do well together."

MORAL.—*Unequal alliances are dangerous to the weaker.*

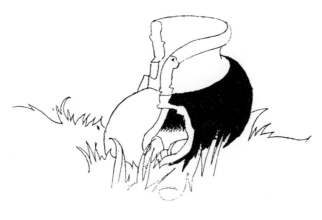

The Dairywoman and the Pot of Milk

A pot of milk upon her cushion'd crown,
Good Peggy hasten'd to the market town;
Short clad and light, with speed she went,
Not fearing any accident;
  Indeed, to be the nimbler tripper,
    Her dress that day,
    The truth to say,
  Was simple petticoat and slipper.
    And, thus bedight,
    Good Peggy, light—
  Her gains already counted—
    Laid out the cash
    At single dash,
  Which to a hundred eggs amounted.
    Three nests she made,
    Which, by the aid
  Of diligence and care were hatch'd.
    "To raise the chicks,
    I'll easy fix,"
  Said she, "beside our cottage thatch'd.
    The fox must get
    More cunning yet,
  Or leave enough to buy a pig.
    With little care
    And any fare,
  He'll grow quite fat and big;
    And then the price
    Will be so nice,

THE POT OF MILK

For which the pork will sell!
  'T will go quite hard
  But in our yard
I'll bring a cow and calf to dwell—
  A calf to frisk among the flock!"
The thought made Peggy do the same;
And down at once the milk-pot came,
  And perish'd with the shock.
Calf, cow, and pig, and chicks, adieu!
Your mistress' face is sad to view;
She gives a tear to fortune spilt;
Then with the downcast look of guilt
Home to her husband empty goes,
Somewhat in danger of his blows.

MORAL.—

Who buildeth not, sometimes, in air
His cots, or seats, or castles fair:
From kings to dairywomen—all—
The wise, the foolish, great and small—
Each thinks his waking dream the best.
Some flattering error fills the breast:
The world with all its wealth is ours,
Its honours, dames, and loveliest bowers.
Instinct with valour, when alone,
I hurl the monarch from his throne;
The people, glad to see him dead,
Elect me monarch in his stead,
And diadems rain on my head.
Some accident then calls me back,
And I'm no more than simple Jack.

The Lion in Love

A LION fell in love with a country lass, and desired her father's consent to have her in marriage. The answer the man gave was churlish enough; he'd never agree to it, he said, upon any terms, to marry his daughter to a beast. Upon this the lion gave him a severe look, which brought the bumpkin, on second thoughts, to strike a bargain with him, upon these conditions: that his teeth should be drawn, and his nails pared; for those were things, he said, of which the foolish girl was terribly afraid. The lion sends for a surgeon immediately to do the work. (What will not love make a body do?) And so soon as the operation was

28

THE LION IN LOVE

over, he goes and claims fulfilment of the father's promise. The countryman, seeing the lion disarmed, plucked up a good heart, and with a swinging cudgel so ordered the matter, that he broke off the match.

MORAL.—*Strength may be overcome by cunning.*

"UPON THE SIGHT OF A SWALLOW"

A Young Man and a Swallow

A prodigal young fellow who had sold his clothes to his very shirt, upon the sight of a swallow that came before her time, made sure that summer was now at hand, and away that went too. There happened after this a fit of bitter cold weather that almost starved both the bird and the spendthrift.

"Well," says the fellow to himself, "this sort of a swallow has been the ruin of us both."

MORAL.—*One swallow does not make a summer.*

31

"TWO BULLS ENGAGED IN SHOCKING BATTLE"

𝕿𝖍𝖊 𝕿𝖜𝖔 𝕭𝖚𝖑𝖑𝖘 𝖆𝖓𝖉 𝖙𝖍𝖊 𝕱𝖗𝖔𝖌

Two bulls engaged in shocking battle,
  Both for a certain heifer's sake,
And lordship over certain cattle;
  A frog began to groan and quake.
    "But what is this to you?"
  Enquired another of the croaking crew.
    "Why, sister, don't you see,
    The end of this will be,
That one of these big brutes will yield,
And then be exiled from the field?
No more permitted on the grass to feed,
He'll forage through our marsh, on rush and reed;
    And while he eats, or chews the cud,
    Will trample on us in the mud.
    Alas! to think how frogs must suffer
    By means of this proud lady heifer!"
This fear was not without good sense.
One bull was beat, and much to their expense;
For, quick retreating to their reedy bower,
He trod on twenty of them in an hour.

MORAL.—

*Of little folks it oft has been the fate
To suffer for the follies of the great.*

Fortune and the Beggar

A beggar was going slowly along a road, grumbling because he was so poor. Yet he thought it strange that so many other people were not contented with their lot.

"Why," said he, "there is a man across the street who is worth hundreds of pounds, yet he is working like a slave to get more. I heard some men talking yesterday about a man who had lost all his money in his desire to become richer than his neighbours. What a silly man he must be! Now I would be contented with a very small sum."

He had not gone many steps farther, when Dame Fortune all at once met him.

"I have long wished to help you," she said. "Hold out your hat and I will fill it with gold. But bear this in mind: if a single coin falls out of it, all the gold will turn to dust."

The beggar was almost beside himself with joy. He took off his hat—a very old one—and Fortune poured into it such a stream of golden coins that the hat soon became very heavy.

"Is that enough?" asked Fortune.

"Not quite enough," said the beggar.

"The hat is beginning to break."

"Never mind, I will risk it."

"Think a moment; have you not enough now?"

"Pour in just a little more."

"There, 't is quite full. Take care."

"Just one more."

34

"A BEGGAR WAS GOING SLOWLY ALONG A ROAD"

"The strain upon the hat was too great. A seam in it burst. The coins fell through the opening and turned to dust. Fortune went away, and the beggar was as poor as before.

"Well, I call that a mean trick," he said. "She might have left me the price of a new hat." And he went on grumbling to the end of his days.

MORAL.—*Those who seek to grasp overmuch often end by losing all.*

A Wolf in a Sheepskin

There is a story of a wolf that wrapped himself up in a sheepskin, and worried lambs for a good while under that disguise; but the shepherd met with him at last, and hung him up, sheepskin and all, for a spectacle and an example. The neighbours made a wonderment of it, and asked him what he meant to hang up his sheep.

"Oh," says he, "that's only the skin of a sheep that was made use of to cover the heart, malice, and body of a wolf that shrouded himself under it!"

MORAL.—*Appearances are sometimes deceptive.*

37

"OLD RODILARD, A CERTAIN CAT"

The Council held by the Rats

Old Rodilard, a certain cat,
   Such havoc of the rats had made,
'T was difficult to find a rat
   With nature's debt unpaid.
The few that did remain,
   To leave their holes afraid,
From usual food abstain,
   Not eating half their fill;
   No wonder no one will.
That one who made of rats his revel,
With rats pass'd not for cat, but devil.
Now, on a day, this dread rat-eater,
Who had a wife, went out to meet her;
And while he held his caterwauling,
The unkill'd rats, their chapter telling,
Discuss'd the point, in grave debate,
How they might shun impending fate.
   Their dean, a prudent rat,
Thought best, and better soon than late,
   To bell the fatal cat;
That, when he took his hunting round,
The rats, well caution'd by the sound,
Might hide in safety underground;
   Indeed he knew no other means.
     And all the rest
     At once confess'd
Their minds were with the dean's.

39

No better plan, they all believed,
Could possibly have been conceived;
No doubt the thing would work right well,
If anyone would hang the bell.
　　But, one by one, said every rat,
　　"I'm not so big a fool as that."
The plan, knock'd up in their respect,
The council closed without effect.

And many a council I have seen,
Or reverend chapter with its dean,
　　That, thus resolving wisely,
　　Fell through like this precisely.

MORAL.—

To argue or refute
　Wise counsellors abound;
The man to execute
　Is harder to be found.

A Fox and a Leopard

AS a leopard was valuing himself upon the lustre of his parti-coloured skin, a fox gave him a jog, and whispered him, that the beauty of the mind was an excellence infinitely above that of a painted outside.

MORAL.—*External beauty is not to be valued for itself.*

Mercury and a Carpenter

A carpenter dropped his axe into a river, and put up a prayer to Mercury to help him to it again. Mercury dived for it, and brought him up a golden one; but that was not it, the fellow said, and so he plunged a second time, and fetched up another of silver. Once more he said that was not it. Mercury tried again, and then up comes an axe with a wooden handle, which, the carpenter said, was the very tool he had lost.

"Well," says Mercury, "thou art so just a poor wretch that I'll give thee all three now for thy honesty."

This story was got into everybody's mouth, and the rumour being spread, it came into a knave's head to try the same experiment over again. And so away goes he, and down he sits, snivelling and yelping, upon the bank of a river, that he had dropped his axe into the water there. Mercury, who was at hand, heard his lamentation, and dipping once again for his axe, as he had done for the other, up he brings him a golden axe, and asks the fellow if that were it.

"Yes, yes," says he, "this is it."

"Oh, thou impudent sot," cries Mercury, "to think of putting tricks upon him that sees through the very heart of thee!"

MORAL.—*Honesty is the best policy.*

MERCURY AND THE CARPENTER

THE DOG SEES HIS SHADOW

𝔄 𝔇𝔬𝔤 𝔞𝔫𝔡 𝔞 𝔖𝔥𝔞𝔡𝔬𝔴

As a dog was crossing a river, with a morsel of good meat in his mouth, he saw, as he thought, another dog under the water upon the very same adventure. He never considered that this was only the reflection of himself, but, out of a greediness to get both pieces of meat, he bites at the shadow, and loses the substance.

MORAL.—*If you covet all you may lose all.*

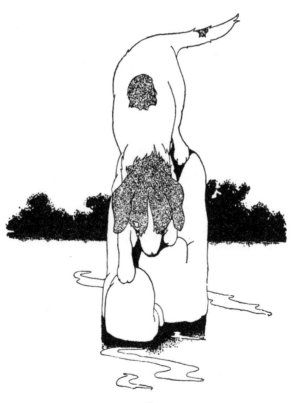

The Cock and the Pearl

A COCK scratch'd up, one day,
A pearl of purest ray,
Which to a jeweller he bore.
"I think it fine," he said;
"But yet a crumb of bread
To me were worth a great
deal more."

So did a dunce inherit
A manuscript of merit,
Which to a publisher he bore.
"'T is good," said he, "I'm
told,
Yet any crown of gold
To me were worth a great
deal more."

MORAL.—*A thing may be worthless to one, which is of great
value to others.*

Two Sides of a Story

"What is the matter?" said Growler to the tabby cat, as she sat moping on the step by the kitchen door.

"Matter enough!" said the cat, turning her head the other way; " our cook talks of hanging me. I wish very much someone would hang her."

"Why, what is the matter?" again asked Growler.

" Has she not beaten me, and called me a thief, and said she would kill me?"

"Dear, dear!" said Growler. "Pray, what has brought that about?"

"Oh, nothing at all! It is her temper. I wonder the mistress does not send her away."

"Well, you see," replied Growler, "she is very useful in the house. You and I might be spared much more easily."

" Not a drop of milk have I had this day," said the cat, "and such a pain in my side!"

" But what is the cause?" asked Growler.

47

"Have I not told you?" said the cat crossly. "It's her temper—oh, what I have had to suffer from it! She blames me for everything that is stolen. Really, I cannot bear it."

Growler was quite angry; but after a little while he asked: "But was there really no cause for her being cross this morning?"

"She was angry because I hurt her feelings," said the cat.

Growler said: "How was it, may I ask?"

"Oh, nothing worth telling—a mere mistake of mine!" replied the cat.

Growler looked at her so strangely that she added: "I took the wrong thing for my breakfast."

"Oh!" said Growler, beginning to understand. "Why, the fact is," continued the cat, "while springing at a mouse, I knocked down a dish, and, not knowing exactly what was in it, I smelt it, and it was rather nice, and——"

"You finished it?" hinted Growler.

"Well, I think I should have done so, if that meddlesome cook had not come in. As it was, I left the head."

"The head of what?" asked Growler.

"What a number of questions you ask!" said the cat.

"Nay, but I should like to know," said Growler.

"Well, then, it was the head of the fish that was meant for dinner."

"Then," said Growler, "say what you please; but since I have heard both sides of the story, I only wonder that the cook did *not* hang you."

MORAL.—*It is necessary to see both sides in a quarrel.*

48

"HOW WAS IT, MAY I ASK?"

The Boy and the Schoolmaster

A BOY, that frolick'd on the banks of
    Seine,
Fell in, and would have found a watery
    grave,
Had not that hand that planteth ne'er
    in vain
A willow planted there, his life to
    save.
While hanging by its branches as he might,
A certain sage preceptor came in sight;
To whom the urchin cried: "Save, or I'm drown'd!"
The master, turning gravely at the sound,
Thought proper for a while to stand aloof,
And give the boy some seasonable reproof.
    "You little wretch! this comes of foolish playing,
    Commands and precepts disobeying.
    A naughty rogue, no doubt, you are,
    Who thus requite your parents' care.
    Alas! their lot I pity much,
    Whom fate condemns to watch o'er such."
    This having coolly said, and more,
    He pulled the drowning lad ashore.
This story hits more marks than you suppose,
All critics, pedants, men of endless prose—
    Three sorts, so richly bless'd with progeny,
    The house is bless'd that doth not lodge any—

May in it see themselves from head to toes.
No matter what the task,
  Their precious tongues much teach;
Their help in need you ask,
  You first must hear them preach.

MORAL.—

Wise counsel is not always wise,
This little tale exemplifies.

𝕬 𝕱𝖔𝖜𝖑𝖊𝖗 𝖆𝖓𝖉 𝖆 𝕻𝖆𝖗𝖙𝖗𝖎𝖉𝖌𝖊

A fowler had taken a partridge, and the bird offered herself to decoy as many of her companions into the snare as she could, upon condition that he would spare her life.

"No," says he, "you shall die the rather for that very reason, because you would be so base as to betray your friends to save yourself."

MORAL.—*A traitor cannot hope to prosper.*

"A FOWLER HAD TAKEN A PARTRIDGE"

A Maid and a Needle

A maid picked a quarrel with her needle, for pricking her fingers.

"Nay," says the needle, "it was none of my fault, neither was it any act of mine; for you forced me to do what I did, and I could not help it."

MORAL.—*We are too often inclined to lay the blame upon others when we hurt ourselves.*

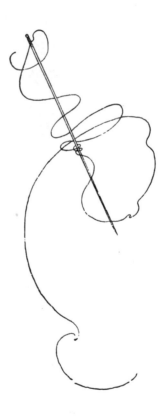

The Bat and the Two Weasels

A blundering bat once stuck her head
Into a wakeful weasel's bed;
Whereat the mistress of the house,
  A deadly foe of rats and mice,
  Was making ready in a trice
To eat the stranger as a mouse.
  "What! do you dare," she said "to creep in
The very bed I sometimes sleep in,
Now, after all the provocation
I 've suffer'd from your thievish nation?
Are you not really then a mouse,
That gnawing pest of every house,
Your special aim to do the cheese ill?
Aye, that you are, or I 'm no weasel."
  "I beg your pardon," said the bat,
  "My kind is very far from that.

55

What! I a mouse! Who told you such a lie?
  Why, ma'am, I am a bird;
  And, if you doubt my word,
Just see the wings with which I fly.
Long live the mice that cleave the sky!"
  These reasons had so fair a show,
  The weasel let the creature go.

By some strange fancy led,
The same wise blunderhead,
But two or three days later,
  Had chosen for her rest
  Another weasel's nest,
This last, of birds a special hater.
  New peril brought this step absurd:
Without a moment's thought or puzzle,
Dame weasel oped her peaked muzzle
  To eat th' intruder as a bird.
"Hold! do not wrong me," cried the bat;
"I 'm truly no such thing as that.
Your eyesight strange conclusions gathers.
What makes a bird, I pray? Its feathers.
  I 'm cousin of the mice and rats.
  Great Jupiter confound the cats!"
The bat, by such adroit replying,
Twice saved herself from dying;

MORAL.—

There 's many a human stranger
Thus turns his coat in danger;
And sings, as suits, where'er he goes,
"God save the king!"—or, "save his foes!"

"THE WEASEL LET THE CREATURE GO"

"A COUNTRY FELLOW HAD THE LUCK TO CAPTURE A HAWK"

A Countryman and a Hawk

A country fellow had the luck to capture a hawk in the pursuit of a pigeon. The hawk pleaded for herself that she never did the countryman any harm, "and therefore, I hope," says she, "that you'll do me none."

"Well," says the countryman, "and pray what wrong did the pigeon ever do you? Now, by the reason of your own argument, you must e'en expect to be treated yourself as you yourself would have treated this pigeon."

MORAL.—*By speaking without thinking we may condemn ourselves out of our own mouths.*

The Hare and the Tortoise

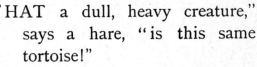

"WHAT a dull, heavy creature," says a hare, "is this same tortoise!"

"And yet," says the tortoise, "I'll run with you for a wager."

No sooner said than done, and the fox, by consent, was to be the judge. They started together, and the tortoise kept jogging on still till he came to the end of the course. The hare laid himself down about midway, and took a nap. "For," says he, "I can fetch up the tortoise when I please." But, as it happened, he overslept himself, for when he awakened, though he scudded away as fast as it was possible, the tortoise got to the post before him, and won the wager.

MORAL.—*Do not be over confident.*

THE TORTOISE WINS THE WAGER

Two Cocks Fighting

Two cocks fought a duel for the mastery of a poultry yard. He that was worsted slunk away into a corner and hid himself; the other takes his flight up to the top of the house, and there, with crowing and clapping of his wings, makes proclamation of his victory. An eagle made a stoop at him in the middle of his exultation, and carried him away. By this accident, the other cock had a good riddance of his rival, took possession of the yard they contended for, and had all his mistresses to himself again.

MORAL.—*A wise and generous enemy will behave modestly over his victory—for fortune is variable.*

'TWO COCKS FOUGHT A DUEL'

𝔄 𝔉𝔯𝔬𝔤 𝔞𝔫𝔡 𝔞 𝔐𝔬𝔲𝔰𝔢

There fell out a quarrel once betwixt the frogs and the mice about the sovereignty of the fens, and whilst two of their companions were disputing it at sword's point, down comes a kite upon them and gobbles up both together, to part the fray.

MORAL.—*When fools quarrel, knaves win.*

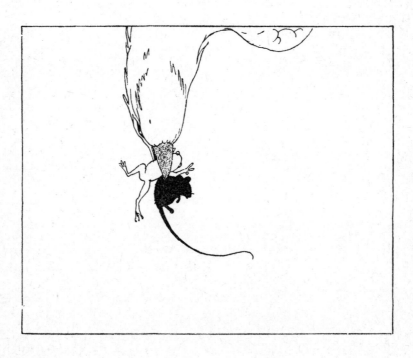

"DOWN COMES A KITE UPON THEM"

The Lion Going to War

THE lion had an enterprise in hand,
    Held a war council, sent his provost-marshal,

And gave the animals a call impartial—

Each, in his way, to serve his high command.

    The elephant should carry on his back
    The tools of war, the mighty public pack,
    And fight in elephantine way and form;

66

The bear should hold himself pre-
  pared to storm;
The fox all secret stratagems should
  fix;
The monkey should amuse the foe
  by tricks.
  "Dismiss," said one, "the block-
    head asses,
And hares, too cowardly and fleet."
"No," said the king, "I use all classes;
Without their aid my force were incom-
  plete.

The ass shall be our
  trumpeter, to scare
Our enemy. And then
  the nimble hare
Our royal bulletins shall homeward bear."

MORAL.—
*A monarch provident
  and wise
Will hold his subjects
  all of consequence,*

*And know in each what talent
  lies.
There's nothing useless to a
  man of sense.*

A Dog and a Cock upon a Journey

A dog and a cock took a journey together. The dog kennelled in the body of a hollow tree, and the cock roosted at night upon the boughs. The cock crowed about midnight, at his usual hour, which brought a fox that was abroad upon the hunt immediately to the tree; and there he stood licking his lips at the cock, and wheedling to get him down. He protested he never heard so angelical a voice sing since he was born, and what would not he do now to hug the creature that had given him so admirable a serenade.

"Pray," says the cock, "speak to the porter below to open the door, and I'll come down to you."

The fox did as he was directed, and the dog promptly seized and worried him.

MORAL.—*It will often be found that those who try to trick others are tricked themselves.*

A Peacock complaining to Juno

The peacock to the queen of heaven
    Complain'd in some such words:—
"Great goddess, you have given
    To me, the laughing-stock of birds,
A voice which fills, by taste quite just,
    All nature with disgust;
Whereas that little paltry thing,
    The nightingale, pours from her throat
    So sweet and ravishing a note,
She bears alone the honours of the spring.

In anger Juno heard,
And cried: "Shame on you, jealous bird!
Grudge you the nightingale her voice,
Who in the rainbow neck rejoice,
Than costliest silks more richly tinted,
In charms of grace and form unstinted,—
  Who strut in kingly pride,
  Your glorious tail spread wide
With brilliants which in sheen do
Outshine the jeweller's bow window?
  Is there a bird beneath the blue
    That has more charms than you?
  No animal in everything can shine.
  By just partition of our gifts divine,
  Each has its full and proper share;
  Among the birds that cleave the air,
The hawk's a swift, the eagle is a brave one,
For omens serves the hoarse old raven,
The rook's of coming ills the prophet;
  And if there's any discontent,
    I've heard not of it.
  Cease, then, your envious complaint;
  Or I, instead of making up your lack,
Will take your boasted plumage from your back."

MORAL.—*Make use of the gifts you have instead of envying those of others.*

THE PEACOCK COMPLAINING

THE UNGRATEFUL KITE

A Bear and Bees

An Eagle and Rabbits

A Mouse and a Kite

A simple mouse had the fortune to be near at hand when a kite was taken in a net. The kite begged of her to try if she could help her out. The mouse gnawed a hole in the net, and set her at liberty,—and the kite ate up the mouse for her pains.

MORAL.—*Save a thief and you may suffer for doing so.*

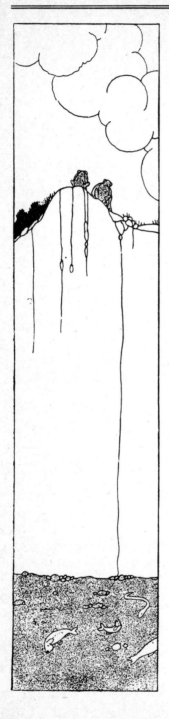

Two Frogs that Wanted Water

Upon the drying of a lake, two frogs were forced to quit it, and seek for water elsewhere. As they were upon the search they discovered a very deep well.

"Come," says one to the other, "let us e'en go down here without looking any farther."

"You say well," says his companion; "but what if the water should fail us here, too? How shall we get out again?"

MORAL.—*It is good advice to look before we leap.*

"THEY DISCOVERED A VERY DEEP WELL"

𝕬 𝕭𝖊𝖆𝖗 𝖆𝖓𝖉 𝕭𝖊𝖊𝖘

A bear was so enraged once at the stinging of a bee, that he ran like mad into the bee-garden, and overturned all the hives in revenge. This outrage brought them out in whole troops upon him, and he came afterwards to bethink himself how much more advisable it had been to pass over one injury than by an unprofitable passion to provoke a thousand.

MORAL.—*It is foolish to avenge one injury by making many enemies.*

TO THE BEE GARDEN

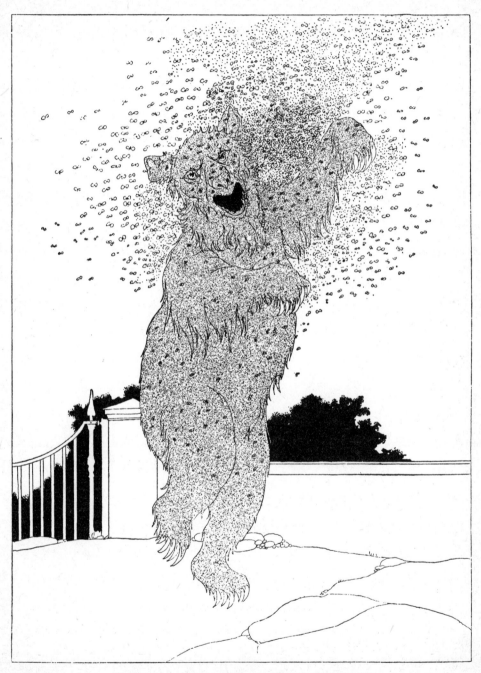

"BROUGHT THEM OUT IN WHOLE TROOPS"

The Man and his Image

A MAN, who had no rivals in
the love
Which to himself he
bore,
Esteem'd his own dear
beauty far above
What earth had seen
before.
More than contented in
his error,
He lived the foe of every mirror.
Officious fate, resolved our lover
From such an illness should recover,
Presented always to his eyes
The mute advisers which the ladies prize;—
Mirrors in parlours, inns, and shops,—
Mirrors the pocket furniture of fops,—
Mirrors on every lady's zone,
From which his face reflected shone.
What could our dear Narcissus do?
From haunts of men he now withdrew,
On purpose that his precious shape
From every mirror might escape.

But in his forest glen alone,
Apart from human trace,
A watercourse,
Of purest source,
While with unconscious gaze

78

HIS IMAGE

He pierced its waveless face,
  Reflected back his own.
Incensed with mingled rage and fright,
He seeks to shun the odious sight;
But yet that mirror sheet, so clear and still,
He cannot leave, do what he will.

MORAL.—

Ere this, my story's drift you plainly see.
From such mistake there is no mortal free.
  That obstinate self-lover
  The human soul doth cover;
The mirror's follies are of others,
In which, as all are genuine brothers,
Each soul may see to life depicted
Itself with just such faults afflicted.

THE STRAIGHT AND CROOKED TREES

𝕿rees 𝕾traight and 𝕮rooked

There was a delicate plantation of trees that were all well-grown, fair, and smooth, save only one dwarf among them that was knotty and crooked; and the rest therefore held it in derision. When the master of the wood had to build a house, he appointed his workmen to supply the timber out of that grove, and to cut down every stick of it that they found fit for service. They did as they were ordered, and did it so well that this ill-favoured tree was left alone.

MORAL.—*Good fortune does not always wait upon the beautiful.*

THE RAVEN ENVIES THE SWAN

82

The Raven and the Swan

A raven had a great wish to be as white as a swan, and fancied to himself that the swan's beauty proceeded chiefly from his frequent washing and diet. The raven, upon this, quitted his former course of life, and betook himself to the lakes and rivers. But as the water did him no good at all for his complexion, so the experiment cost him his life too for want of proper food.

MORAL.—*Black is black and white is white.*

𝔄 𝔏𝔞𝔡 ℜ𝔬𝔟𝔟𝔦𝔫𝔤 𝔞𝔫 𝔒𝔯𝔠𝔥𝔞𝔯𝔡

An old man found a boy robbing his orchard.

"Sirrah," says he, "come down the tree, and don't steal my apples."

The lad never minded him, but went on with his work.

"Well," says the master of the ground, "they say there are charms in herbs, as well as in words," and so he threw a handful of grass at him, which was so ridiculous that the young thief took the old man to be silly.

"But, in conclusion, if neither words nor herbs will do," says he, "I'll try what may be done with stones, for they say there's virtue in them too," and that way he did his work.

MORAL.—*Those who will not amend through instruction must be made to do so by punishment.*

"THREW A HANDFUL OF GRASS AT HIM"

The Dragon with Many Heads, and the Dragon with Many Tails

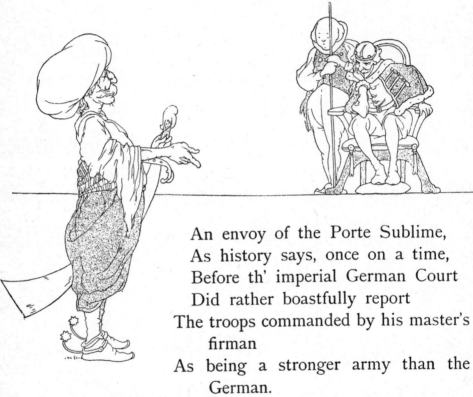

An envoy of the Porte Sublime,
As history says, once on a time,
Before th' imperial German Court
Did rather boastfully report
The troops commanded by his master's
    firman
As being a stronger army than the
    German.
To which replied a Dutch attendant:
"Our prince has more than one dependant
Who keeps an army at his own expense."
   The Turk, a man of sense,
   Rejoin'd: "I am aware
What power your emperor's servants share.
It brings to mind a tale both strange and true,
A thing which once, myself, I chanced to view.

THE TWO DRAGONS

I saw come darting through a hedge,
Which fortified a rocky ledge,
A hydra's hundred heads; and in a trice
   My blood was turning into ice.
   But less the harm than terror;
   The body came no nearer,
   Nor could, unless it had been sunder'd
   To parts at least a hundred.
   While musing deeply on this sight,
   Another dragon came to light,

Who single head avails
To lead a hundred tails;
And, seized with juster fright,
I saw him pass into the hedge,
Head, body, tails—a wedge
Of living and resistless powers.
The other was your emperor's force; this ours."

MORAL.—*One leader is stronger than many leaders.*

The Fox and the Grapes

The Frogs Choose a King

An Ass, a Lion, and a Cock

As a cock and an ass were feeding together, up comes a lion open mouthed toward the ass. The cock presently cries out; away scours the lion, and the ass after him. Now it was the crowing of the cock that frightened the lion, not the braying of the ass, as that stupid animal vainly fancied to himself; for so soon as ever they were out of the hearing of the cock, the lion turned short upon him, and tore him to pieces, with these words in his mouth: "Let never any creature hereafter that has not the courage of a hare provoke a lion."

MORAL.—*The fool is wise and brave only in his own conceit, and suffers accordingly.*

The Peach, Apple, and Blackberry

There happened a controversy once betwixt a peach and an apple which was the fairer fruit of the two. They were so loud in their discourse that a blackberry from the next hedge overheard them.

"Come," says the blackberry, "we are all friends, and pray let's have no jangling among ourselves."

MORAL.—*It is idle to dispute about trival matters.*

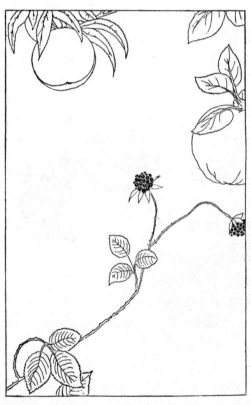

The Raven

A raven, while with glossy breast
Her new-laid eggs she fondly pressed,
And on her wickerwork high mounted,
Her chickens prematurely counted
(A fault philosophers might blame
If quite exempted from the same),
Enjoy'd at ease the genial day.
'T was April as the bumpkins say:
The legislature called it May.
But suddenly a wind as high
As ever swept a wintry sky
Shook the young leaves about her
　　ears,
And filled her with a thousand fears,
Lest the rude blast should snap the
　　bow,
And spread her golden hopes below.
But just at eve the blowing weather
And all her fears were hushed to-
　　gether.
And now, quoth poor unthinking
　　Ralph,
'T is over and the brood is safe;
(For Ravens — though, as birds of
　　omen,
They teach both conj'rers and old
　　women

91

To tell us what is to befall—
Can't prophesy themselves at all).
The morning came, when neighbour Hodge,
Who long had marked her airy lodge,
And destin'd all the treasure there
A gift to his expecting fair,
Climb'd like a squirrel to his dray,
And bore the worthless prize away.

MORAL.—

*'Tis providence alone secures
In every change, but mine and yours.
Safety consists not in escape
From dangers of a frightful shape;
An earthquake may be bid to spare
A man that's strangled by a hair.
Fate steals along with silent tread,
Found oft'nest in what least we dread,
Frowns in the storm with angry brow,
But in the sunshine strikes the blow.*

"CLIMB'D LIKE A SQUIRREL"

The Man and a Satyr

THERE was a man and a satyr that kept much together. The man put his fingers one day to his mouth and blew upon them.

"What's that for?" says the satyr.

"Why," says he, "my hands are extremely cold, and I do it to warm them."

The satyr, at another time, found this man blowing his porridge.

"And, pray," says he, "what's the meaning of that now?"

"Oh," says the man, "my porridge is hot, and I do it to cool it!"

"Nay," says the satyr, "if you have a trick of blowing hot and cold out of the same mouth, I have done with you."

MORAL.—*It is foolish to judge hastily.*

THE SATYR IS SURPRISED

𝕴𝖓𝖉𝖚𝖘𝖙𝖗𝖞 𝖆𝖓𝖉 𝕾𝖑𝖔𝖙𝖍

A man was asking a lazy young fellow what made him lie in bed so long?

"Why," says he, "I am hearing of causes every morning; that is to say, I have two lasses at my bedside so soon as ever I wake. Their names are Industry and Sloth. One bids me get up, the other bids me lie still, and so they give me twenty reasons why I should rise, and why I should not. It is the part in the meantime of a just judge to hear what can be said on both sides; and before the cause is over, it is time to go to dinner."

MORAL.—*It is idle to waste in deliberation time which should be spent in doing.*

A LAZY YOUNG FELLOW

"AND CARRIED THEM AWAY"

An Eagle and Rabbits

There was an eagle that took a number of young rabbits and carried them away to her young. The mother followed her with tears in her eyes, begging her in the name of all those powers that take care of the innocent and oppressed to have compassion upon her miserable children. But she, in an outrage of pride and indignation, tore them to pieces. The rabbit, upon this, convenes a whole warren, tells her story, and advises upon a revenge. "For Justice," says she, "will never suffer so barbarous a cruelty to escape unpunished." They debated the matter, and came to a unanimous resolve upon the question, that there was no way of paying the eagle in her kind but by undermining the tree in the top of which she dwelt. So they all fell to work at the roots of the tree, and left it so little foothold, that the first blast of wind laid it flat upon the ground, nest, eagles, and all. Some of them were killed with the fall, others were eaten up by birds and beasts of prey, and the rabbit had the comfort at last of destroying the eagle's children in revenge for her own.

MORAL.—*The weak combined may overthrow the powerful.*

𝔄 𝔚𝔬𝔩𝔣 𝔞𝔫𝔡 𝔞 𝔏𝔞𝔪𝔟

As a wolf was lapping at the head of a fountain, he spied a lamb, paddling at the same time, a good way off down the stream. The wolf had no sooner the prey in his eye than away he runs openmouth to it.

"Villain," says he, "how dare you lie muddling the water that I'm a-drinking?"

"Indeed," says the poor lamb, "I did not think that my drinking there below could have fouled your water so far above."

"Nay," says the other, "you'll never leave your chopping of logic till your skin is turned over your ears, as your father's was, a matter of six months ago, for prating at this saucy rate. You remember it full well, sirrah!"

"If you'll believe me, sir," quoth the innocent lamb, with fear and trembling, "I was not come into the world then."

"Why, thou impudence," cries the wolf, "hast thou neither shame nor conscience? But it runs in the blood of your whole race, sirrah, to hate our family; and therefore, since Fortune has brought us together so conveniently, you shall e'en pay some of your forefathers' scores before you and I part;" and so, without more ado, he leapt at the throat of the miserable, helpless lamb, and tore him immediately to pieces.

MORAL.—*Innocence is no protection against the cruelty of a tyrant*

The Fisherman and the Little Fish

A fisherman, who all the seashore drain'd,
While he with slender rod sweet life maintain'd,
Once caught with horsehair line a tiny fish,
Ill-suited for the frying-pan or dish.
The gasping fish its captor thus besought:
"What am I worth? For what shall I be bought?
I 'm not half-grown! whom on yon rocky shore
My mother in the seaweed lately bore.
Now let me go; oh, kill me not in vain!
And you shall catch me when you come again,
On seaweed good ere then grown large and fine,
And meet to grace a board where rich men dine."
As thus she prayed, she raised a piteous moan,
And panted much; but the old man was stone.
Vain was her hope with winning words to plead;
He said, while piercing her with ruthless reed:
"*Who holds not fast a small but certain prize*
Is but a fool, to seek uncertainties."

"ONCE CAUGHT WITH HORSEHAIR LINE A TINY FISH"

The Fox and the Grapes

There was a time when a fox would have ventured as far for a bunch of grapes as for a shoulder of mutton, and it was a fox of those days, and of that taste, that stood gaping under a vine, and licking his lips at a most delicious cluster of grapes that he had spied out there; he tried a hundred and a hundred leaps at it, till at last, when he was weary, and found that there was no good to be done, "Hang 'em," said he, "they are sour," and so away he went, turning off the disappointment with a jest.

MORAL.—*It is easy to find an excuse for disappointment*

The Cockerel, the Cat, and the Young Mouse

A youthful mouse, not up to trap,
Had almost met a sad mishap.
The story hear him thus relate,
    With great importance, to his mother:
"I pass'd the mountain bounds of this estate,
    And off was trotting on another,
Like some young rat with naught to do
But see things wonderful and new,
When two strange creatures came in view.
The one was mild, benign, and gracious;
The other, turbulent, rapacious,
With voice terrific, shrill, and rough,
And on his head a bit of stuff
That look'd like raw and bloody meat,
Raised up a sort of arms, and beat
The air, as if he meant to fly,
And bore his plumy tail on high."

A cock, that just began to crow,
    As if some nondescript,
    From far New Holland shipp'd,
Was what our mouseling pictured so.
"He beat his arms," said he, "and raised his voice,
    And made so terrible a noise,
That I, who, thanks to Heaven, may justly boast
    Myself as bold as any mouse,
Scud off (his voice would even scare a ghost!),
    And cursed himself and all his house;

For, but for him, I should have stayed,
And doubtless an acquaintance made
With her who seem'd so mild and good.
Like us, in velvet cloak and hood,
She wears a tail that's full of grace,
A very sweet and humble face,—
No mouse more kindness could desire,—
And yet her eye is full of fire.
I do believe the lovely creature
A friend of rats and mice by nature.
Her ears, though, like herself, they're bigger,
Are just like ours in form and figure.
To her I was approaching, when,
Aloft on what appear'd his den,
The other scream'd—and off I fled."
"My son," his cautious mother said,
  "That sweet one was the cat,
  The mortal foe of mouse and rat,
  Who seeks, by smooth deceit,
  Her appetite to treat.
So far the other is from that,
    We yet may eat
    His dainty meat;
Whereas the cruel cat,
When'er she can, devours
No other meat than ours."

MORAL.—

Remember, while you live,
It is by looks that men deceive.

"THE OTHER SCREAMED—AND OFF I FLED"

The Bear and the Amateur Gardener

A certain mountain bear, unlick'd and rude,
By fate confined within a lonely wood,
A new Bellerophon, whose life
Knew neither comrade, friend, nor wife,—
Became insane; for reason, as we term it,
Dwells never long with any hermit.
'T is good to mix in good society,
Obeying laws of due propriety;
And better yet to be alone;
But both are ills when overdone.
No animal had business where
All grimly dwelt our hermit bear;
Hence, bearish as he was, he grew
Heartsick, and long'd for something new.
While he to sadness was addicted,
  An aged man, not far from there,
Was by the same disease afflicted.
  A garden was his favourite care—
  Sweet Flora's priesthood, light and fair,
And eke Pomona's—ripe and red
The presents that her fingers shed.
These two employments, true, are sweet
When made so by some friend discreet.
The gardens, gaily as they look,
Talk not (except in this my book);
So, tiring of the deaf and dumb,
Our man each morning left his home

108

"A GARDEN WAS HIS FAVOURITE CARE"

Some company to seek,
That had the power to speak.
The bear, with thoughts the same,
Down from his mountain came;
And in a solitary place,
They met each other, face to face.
It would have made the boldest tremble;
What did our man? To play the Gascon
The safest seem'd. He put the mask on,
His fear contriving to dissemble.
The bear, unused to compliment,
Growl'd bluntly, but with good intent,
"Come home with me." The man replied:
"Sir Bear, my lodgings, nearer by,
In yonder garden you may spy,
Where, if you'll honour me the while,
We'll break our fast in rural style.
I've fruits and milk—unworthy fare,
It may be, for a wealthy bear;
But then I offer what I have."
The bear accepts, with visage grave,
But not unpleased; and on their way,
They grow familiar, friendly, gay.
Arrived, you see them side by side,
As if their friendship had been tried.
To a companion so absurd
Blank solitude were well preferr'd;
Yet, as the bear scarce spoke a word,
The man was left quite at his leisure
To trim his garden at his pleasure.

Sir Bruin hunted—always brought
His friend whatever game he caught;
But chiefly aim'd at driving flies—
Those bold and shameless parasites,
That vex us with their ceaseless bites—
From off our gardener's face and eyes.
One day, while stretch'd upon the ground
The old man lay, in sleep profound,
A fly that buzz'd around his nose—
And bit it sometimes, I suppose—
Put Bruin sadly to his trumps.
At last, determined, up he jumps;
" I 'll stop thy noisy buzzing now,"
Says he; " I know precisely how."
    No sooner said than done.
    He seized a paving-stone;
And by his *modus operandi*
Did both the fly and man die.

MORAL.—

A foolish friend may cause more woe
Than could, indeed, the wisest foe.

The Crows and a Mussel

There was once a Royston-crow that was battering upon a mussel, and could not break the shell to get at the fish. A carrion crow comes up and tells him that what he could not do by force he might do by stratagem.

"Take this mussel up in the air," says the crow, "as high as you can carry it, and then let him fall upon that rock there. His own weight, you shall see, will break him."

The Royston-crow took his advice, and it succeeded accordingly. But while the one was up in the air, the other stood waiting upon the ground, and flew away with the fish.

MORAL.—*Some people are kind to their neighbours for their own sakes.*

"THE ROYSTON-CROW TOOK HIS ADVICE"

Jupiter and a Herdsman

A herdsman that had lost a calf out of his grounds, sent up and down after it; and when he could get no tidings of it he betook himself at last to his prayers.

"Great Jupiter," says he, "do but show me the thief that stole my calf, and I'll give thee a kid for a sacrifice."

The word was no sooner passed but the thief appeared; which was indeed a lion. This discovery put him to his prayers once again.

"I have not forgotten my vow," says he, "but now thou hast brought me to the thief I'll make that kid a bull if thou wilt but set me quit of him again."

MORAL.—*We cannot be too careful in the making of vows and promises.*

The Cat, the Weasel, and the Young Rabbit

John Rabbit's palace underground
Was once by Goody Weasel found.
She, sly of heart, resolved to seize
The place, and did so at her ease.
She took possession while its lord
Was absent on the dewy sward,
Intent upon his usual sport,
A courtier at Aurora's Court.
When he had browsed his fill of clover
And cut his pranks all nicely over,
Home Johny came to take his drowse,
All snug within his cellar-house.
The weasel's nose he came to see,
 Outsticking through the open door.
"Ye gods of hospitality!"
 Exclaim'd the creature, vexèd sore,
"Must I give up my father's lodge?
 Ho, Madam Weasel, please to budge,
Or, quicker than a weasel's dodge,
 I'll call the rats to pay their grudge!"
The sharp-nosed lady made reply,
 That she was first to occupy.
The cause of war was surely small—
A house where only one could crawl!
And though it were a vast domain,
Said she, "I'd like to know what will
Could grant to John perpetual reign,—

The son of Peter or of Bill,—
More than to Paul, or even me."
John Rabbit spoke—great lawyer he—
Of custom, usage, as the law,
   Whereby the house, from sire to son,
As well as all its store of straw,
   From Peter came at length to John.
Who could present a claim so good
As he, the first possessor, could?
"Now," said the dame, "let's drop dispute,
   And go before Raminagrobis;
Who'll judge, not only in this suit,
   But tell us truly whose the globe is."
This person was a hermit cat,
   A cat that played the hypocrite,
A saintly mouser, sleek and fat,
   An arbiter of keenest wit.
John Rabbit in the judge concurr'd,
And off went both their case to broach
Before his majesty, the furr'd.
   Said Clapperclaw: "My kits, approach,
And put your noses to my ears:
I'm deaf, almost, by weight of years."
And so they did, not fearing aught.
   The good apostle, Clapperclaw,
   Then laid on each a well-arm'd paw,
And both to an agreement brought,
   By virtue of his tusked jaw.

This brings to mind the fate
Of little kings before the great.

"SAID CLAPPERCLAW: 'MY KITS, APPROACH'"

𝕬 𝕸an that carried his 𝕻lough to ease his 𝕺xen

A peasant that had ploughed himself and his oxen quite a-weary mounted an ass, with the plough before him, and sent the oxen to dinner. The poor ass, he found, was ready to sink under the load, and so he took up the plough, and laid it upon his own shoulders.

"Now," says he to the ass, "thou mayest carry me well enough, when I carry the plough."

MORAL.—*It is better to reason carefully than quickly.*

"THOU MAYEST CARRY ME WELL ENOUGH, WHEN I CARRY THE PLOUGH"

119

𝕿𝖍𝖊 𝕳𝖊𝖗𝖔𝖓

One day—no matter when or where—
A long-legg'd heron chanced to fare
  By a certain river's brink,
  With his long, sharp beak
  Helved on his slender neck:
'T was a fish-spear, you might think.
The water was clear and still,
The carp and the pike there at will
  Pursued their silent fun,
  Turning up, ever and anon,
  A golden side to the sun.
With ease might the heron have made
Great profits in his fishing trade.
So near came the scaly fry,
They might be caught by the passer-by.
But he thought he better might
Wait for a better appetite—
For he lived by rule, and could not eat,
Except at his hours, the best of meat.
Anon his appetite return'd once more;
So, approaching again the shore,
He saw some tench taking their leaps,
  Now and then, from their lowest deeps.
  With as dainty taste as Horace's rat,
  He turn'd away from such food as that.
 "What, tench for a heron! poh!
  I scorn the thought, and let them go."
The tench refused, there came a gudgeon;
"For all that," said the bird, "I budge on.

THE HERON

I 'll ne'er open my beak, if the gods please,
For such mean little fishes as these."
   He did it for less;
   For it came to pass,
That not another fish could he see;
And, at last, so hungry was he,
That he thought it of some avail
To find on the bank a single snail.

MORAL.—

Such is the sure result
Of being too difficult.
Would you be strong, and great,
Learn to accommodate.
Get what you can, and trust for the rest;
The whole is oft lost by seeking the best.
Above all things, beware of disdain;
Where, at most, you have little to gain.
The people are many that make
Every day this sad mistake.
'T is not for the herons I put the case,
Ye featherless people, of human race.
—List to another tale as true,
And you 'll hear the lesson brought home to you.

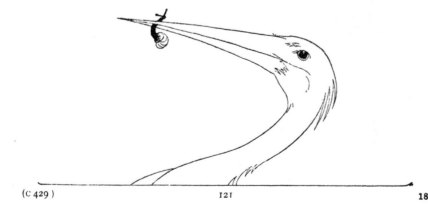

The Cat and the Rat

Four creatures, wont to prowl—
 Sly Grab-and-scratch, the cat,
Grave Evil-bode, the owl,
 Thief Nibble-stitch, the rat,
And Madam Weasel, prim and
 fine—
Inhabited a rotten pine.
A man their home discover'd there,
And set, one night, a cunning
 snare.
 The cat, a noted early riser,
 Went forth, at break of day,
 To hunt her usual prey.
 Not much the wiser
 For morning's feeble ray,
The noose did suddenly surprise
 her.
 Waked by her strangling cry,
 Grey Nibble-stitch drew nigh:
 As full of joy was he
 As of despair was she;
 For in the noose he saw
 His foe of mortal paw.
"Dear friend," said Mrs. Grab-
 and-scratch,
"Do, pray, this cursed cord de-
 tach.
 I 've always known your skill,

122

"THE NOOSE DID SUDDENLY SURPRISE HER"

And often your goodwill;
Now help me from this worst of snares,
In which I fell at unawares.
   'T is by a sacred right,
    You, sole of all your race,
    By special love and grace,
   Have been my favourite—
    The darling of my eyes.
   'T was order'd by celestial cares,
No doubt; I thank the blessed skies,
  That, going out to say my prayers,
As cats devout each morning do,
This net has made me pray to you.
Come, fall to work upon the cord."
Replied the rat: "And what reward
   Shall pay me, if I dare?"
   "Why," said the cat, "I swear
   To be your firm ally:
   Henceforth, eternally,
   These powerful claws are yours,
   Which safe your life insures.
I 'll guard from quadruped and fowl;
I 'll eat the weasel and the owl."
   "Ah," cried the rat, "you fool!
I 'm quite too wise to be your tool."
He said, and sought his snug retreat,
Close at the rotten pine tree's feet,
Where plump he did the weasel meet;
Whom shunning by a happy dodge,
He climb'd the hollow trunk to lodge;

And there the savage owl he saw.
Necessity became his law,
And down he went, the rope to gnaw.
Strand after strand in two he bit,
And freed, at last, the hypocrite.
That moment came the man in sight;
The new allies took hasty flight.

A good while after that,
Our liberated cat
Espied her favourite rat,
Quite out of reach, and on his guard.
"My friend," said she, "I take your shyness hard;
Your caution wrongs my gratitude;
Approach, and greet your stanch ally.
Do you suppose, dear rat, that I
Forget the solemn oath I mew'd!"
"Do I forget," the rat replied,
"To what your nature is allied?
To thankfulness, or even pity,
Can cats be ever bound by treaty?"

MORAL.—

Alliance from necessity
Is safe just while it has to be.

The Stag, the Horse and his Rider

A HORSE, who had never yet been ridden, was feeding in freedom in a grassy plain, when he observed that a broad-horned stag was grazing by him. He thought he had no reason to fear, but that the plain would produce grass enough for them both, and that he had this advantage over the stag, that he might find his food in the thickets or woods, where the horns of the other would not permit him to look for his; yet desiring to have both plain and woods to himself, he besought a man to get up on his back, and to pursue and kill the swift-footed stag. This the man readily consented to do, but told the horse that, for their greater ease and pleasure, it would be necessary for him to be bridled and saddled. The horse, hoping the more certainly to kill the stag, and thereby to range sole

126

"THUS THEY PURSUED THE STAG"

lord and master over all the grassy soil, willingly yielded to it, and opened his mouth to receive the bit, and offered his back to the saddle. Thus they pursued the stag, and the poor beast was caught and slain. Then the horse, believing the rider had obtained his ends as well as himself, desired him to alight and ease him of his heavy weight. But the man answered, That he had not killed the stag only for his interest, but to make himself merry with it among his friends, and that he must be contented to carry him and the stag too home to his house. The horse, though loath, was forced to do so, and then desired the man a second time to get off his back. But he replied again, That he must carry him to fetch some bread to eat with his venison; adding withal, that he now saw how serviceable a beast a horse was to man, either for carrying or drawing their heavy burdens, but that they were chiefly necessary in horse-mills; and that, in short, it was very reasonable that beasts should be tamed, and taught to obey men. Upon this the horse began to kick and fling as he had been mad, thinking to throw his rider; but he sate fast in the saddle, and plied him so furiously with whip and spur, that the horse was forced to submit, and suffered himself to be harnessed in a horse-mill, where ever afterwards he was kept to hard labour, and had no more food allowed him than so much as that man, his then master, thought fit.

MORAL.—*It is foolish to enlist a stronger ally to help one to attain a selfish end.*

The Fishes and the Frying-pan

A cook was frying a dish of live fish, and so soon as ever they felt the heat of the pan, "There's no enduring of this," cried one, and so they all leapt into the fire, and instead of mending the matter they were worse now than before.

MORAL.—*It is easy to go from bad to worse.*

𝔗𝔥𝔢 𝔉𝔯𝔬𝔤𝔰 𝔠𝔥𝔬𝔬𝔰𝔢 𝔞 𝔎𝔦𝔫𝔤

In days of old, when the frogs were all at liberty in the lakes, and grown quite weary of living without government, they petitioned Jupiter for a king, to the end that there might be some distinction of good and evil, by certain equitable rules and methods of reward and punishment. Jupiter, who knew the vanity of their hearts, threw them down a log for their governor; which, upon the first dash, frightened all of them into the mud for the very fear of it. This panic terror kept them in awe for a while, till in good time one frog, bolder than the rest, put up his head, and looked about him, to see how matters went with their new king. Upon this, he calls his fellow subjects together, opens the truth of the case, and nothing would serve them then but riding a-top of him; insomuch that the dread they were in before is now turned into insolence and tumult. This king, they said, was too tame for them, and Jupiter must needs be entreated to send them another. He did so, but authors are divided upon it, whether it was a stork or a serpent; though whichever of the two it was, he left them neither liberty nor property, but made a prey of his subjects. Such was their condition in fine, that they sent Mercury to Jupiter yet once again for another king, whose answer was this: "They that will not be contented when they are well, must be patient when things are amiss with them; and people had better rest where they are, than go farther, and fare worse."

MORAL.—*In changing for the sake of changing we may easily go from bad to worse.*

130

"MADE A PREY OF HIS SUBJECTS"

THE DOLPHIN AND THE APE

An Ape and a Dolphin

In days of old, when people carried apes and puppies with them to sea for their entertainment, there was an ape aboard a vessel that was wrecked in a very bad storm. As the crew were struggling in the water, a dolphin, mistaking the ape for a man, offered to take him to the land. As they were travelling along, the dolphin asked the ape whether he was an Athenian or not. Yes, answered the ape, saying that he was of a very ancient family there.

"Why, then," says the dolphin, "you know Piræus."

"Oh, exceedingly well!" says the ape, mistaking the name of a place for the name of a man. "Why, Piræus is my very particular good friend."

The dolphin was at this so indignant at the impudence of the pretender that he let him slip off and left him to drown.

MORAL.—*Idle bragging is likely to have an ill ending.*

The Two Buckets

Two buckets in an ancient well
  Got talking once together,
And after sundry wise remarks—
  No doubt about the weather—
"Look here!" quoth one; "this life we lead
  I don't exactly like;
Upon my word, I'm half-inclined
  To venture on a strike.
For—do you mind?—however full
  We both come up the well,
We go down empty—always shall,
  For ought that I can tell."

"That's true," the other said; "but then—
  The way it looks to me—
However empty we go down
  We come up full, you see."
Wise little bucket! If we each
  Would look at life that way,
Would dwarf its ills, and magnify
  Its blessings day by day,
The world would be a happier place,
  Since we should all decide
Only the buckets full to count,
  And let the empty slide.

MORAL.—*Look upon the bright side of things.*

THE TWO BUCKETS

"TWO BUCKETS IN AN ANCIENT WELL"

135

The Use of Knowledge

Between two citizens
  A controversy grew.
The one was poor, but much he knew:
The other, rich, with little sense,
Claim'd that, in point of excellence,
The merely wise should bow the knee
To all such money'd men as he.
The merely fools, he should have said;
For why should wealth hold up its head
When merit from its side hath fled?
  " My friend," quoth Bloated-purse,
      To his reverse,
  " You think yourself considerable.
Pray, tell me, do you keep a table?
What comes of this incessant reading,
In point of lodging, clothing, feeding?
It gives one, true, the highest chamber,
One coat for June and for December,
His shadow for his sole attendant,
And hunger always in th' ascendant.
  What profits he his country, too,
  Who scarcely ever spends a sou—
Will, haply, be a public charge?
Who profits more the state at large,
Than he whose luxuries dispense
Among the people wealth immense?
We set the streams of life a-flowing;
We set all sorts of trades a-going,

THE USE OF KNOWLEDGE

The spinner, weaver, sewer, vendor,
And many a wearer, fair and tender,
All live and flourish on the spender—
As do, indeed, the reverend rooks
Who waste their time in making books."
  These words, so full of impudence,
  Received their proper recompense.
The man of letters held his peace,
Though much he might have said with ease.
A war avenged him soon and well;
In it their common city fell.
Both fled abroad; the ignorant,
By fortune thus brought down to want,
Was treated everywhere with scorn,
And roamed about, a wretch forlorn;
Whereas the scholar, everywhere,
Was nourish'd by the public care.

MORAL.—

Let fools the studious despise;
There's nothing lost by being wise.

𝕬 Countryman and a 𝕭oar

A COUNTRYMAN caught a boar in his corn once, and cut off one of his ears. He caught him a second time, and cut off the other. He caught him a third time, and made a present of him to his landlord. Upon the opening of his head they found he had no brains, and everybody fell a wondering and discoursing upon it.

" Sir," says the clown, " if this boar had had any brains, he would have taken the loss of both his ears for a warning never to come into my corn again."

MORAL.—*He must be a fool who will take no warning.*

THE DISCUSSION

The Monkey and the Cat

SLY Bertrand and Ratto in com-
pany sat
(The one was a monkey, the
other a cat),
Co-servants and lodgers:
More mischievous codgers
Ne'er mess'd from a platter,
since platters were flat.
Was anything wrong in the
house or about it,
The neighbours were blameless
—no mortal could doubt it;
For Bertrand was thievish, and Ratto so nice,
More attentive to cheese than he was to the mice.
One day the two plunderers sat by the fire,
Where chestnuts were roasting, with looks of desire.
To steal them would be a right noble affair.
A double inducement our heroes drew there—
'T would benefit them, could they swallow their fill,
And then 't would occasion to somebody ill.
Said Bertrand to Ratto: " My brother, to-day
Exhibit your powers in a masterly way,
And take me these chestnuts, I pray.
Which were I but otherwise fitted
(As I am ingeniously witted)
For pulling things out of the flame,
Would stand but a pitiful game."

"SLY BERTRAND AND RATTO IN COMPANY SAT"

"'T is done," replied Ratto, all prompt to obey,
And thrust out his paw in a delicate way.
  First giving the ashes a scratch,
  He open'd the coveted batch;
  Then lightly and quickly impinging,
  He drew out, in spite of the singeing,
One after another, the chestnuts at last—
While Bertrand contrived to devour them as fast.
  A servant girl enters. Adieu to the fun.
  Our Ratto was hardly contented, says one.—

MORAL.—

No more are the princes, by flattery paid
For furnishing help in a different trade,
  And burning their fingers to bring
  More power to some mightier king.

A Lion and a Bear

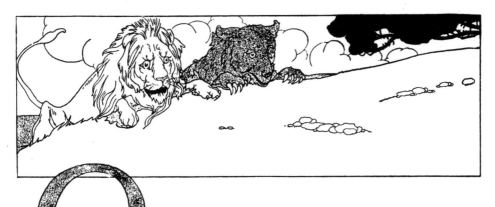

ONCE a lion and a bear had a fawn be-twixt them, and were at it tooth and nail which of the two should carry it off. They fought it out till they were glad to lie down and take breath. In which instant, a fox passing that way, and finding how the case stood with the combatants, seized upon the fawn for his own use, and scampered away with it. The lion and the bear saw the whole action, but, not being in condition to rise and hinder it, they passed this reflection upon the whole matter: Here have we been worrying one another who should have the booty, till this fox has robbed us both of it.

MORAL.—*It is the foolishness of others that gives the knave his opportunity.*

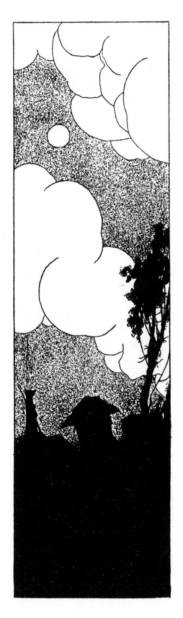

A Wolf Turned Shepherd

There was a crafty wolf that dressed himself up like a shepherd, with his crook, and all his trade about him, to the very pipe and posture. This masquerade succeeded so well that in the dead of the night once, when the men and their dogs were all fast asleep, he would be offering at the shepherd's voice and call too. But there was something of a howl in the tone that the country presently took an alarm at, and so they fell in upon him in his disguise, when he was so shackled and hampered that he could neither fight nor fly.

MORAL.—*The cleverest disguise is liable to discovery.*

THE CRAFTY WOLF TURNS SHEPHERD

𝕿𝖜𝖔 𝕿𝖗𝖆𝖛𝖊𝖑𝖑𝖊𝖗𝖘 𝕱𝖎𝖓𝖉 𝖆𝖓 𝕺𝖞𝖘𝖙𝖊𝖗

As two men were walking by the seaside at low water, they saw an oyster, and they both pointed at it together. The one stoops to pick it up, the other gives him a push, and tells him: "'Tis not yet decided whether it shall be yours or mine."

While they were disputing their title to it, a third man comes that way, and to him they referred the matter which of the two had the better right to the oyster. The arbitrator very gravely takes out his knife, and opens it; the plaintiff and defendant at the same time gaping at the man to see what would come of it: He loosens the fish, gulps it down, and, so soon as ever the morsel was gone, wipes his mouth and pronounces judgment.

"My masters," says he, with the voice of authority, "the Court has ordered each of you a shell, without costs, and so pray go home again and live peaceably among your neighbours."

MORAL.—*If two cannot agree, they may readily be despoiled by a third.*

The Foolish Chicken

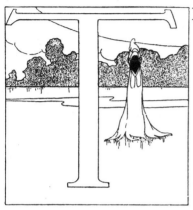

HERE was a round pond, and a
pretty pond too;
About it white daisies and violets
grew,
And dark weeping willows, that
stoop to the ground,
Dipped in their long branches,
and shaded it round.

A party of ducks to this pond
would repair,
To feast on the green waterweeds that grew there;
Indeed, the assembly would frequently meet
To discuss their affairs in this pleasant retreat.

Now the subjects on which they were wont to converse
I'm sorry I cannot include in my verse;
For, though I've oft listened in hopes of discerning,
I own 'tis a matter that baffles my learning.

One day a young chicken, that lived thereabout,
Stood watching to see the ducks pass in and out,
Now standing tail upward, now diving below.
She thought: "Of all things I should like to do so."

So the poor silly chick was determined to try;
She thought 'twas as easy to swim as to fly.

147

Though her mother had told her she must not go near,
She foolishly thought there was nothing to fear.

"My feet, wings, and feathers, for aught I can see,
As good as the ducks are for swimming," said she;
"Though *my* beak is pointed, and *their* beaks are round,
Is that any reason that I should be drowned?

"Why should I not swim, then, as well as a duck?
I think I shall venture, and e'en try my luck.
For," said she, spite of all that her mother had taught her,
"I'm really remarkably fond of the water."

So in this poor ignorant animal flew,
But soon found her dear mother's warnings were true.
She splashed, and she dashed, and she turned herself round,
And heartily wished herself safe on the ground.

But now 't was too late to begin to repent;
The harder she struggled the deeper she went.
And when every effort had vainly been tried,
She slowly sank down to the bottom and died.

The ducks, I perceived, began loudly to quack
When they saw the poor fowl floating dead on its back;
And, by their grave gestures and looks, 't was apparent
They discoursed on the sin of not minding a parent.

MORAL.—*It is foolish not to learn from the experience of others.*

"WHY SHOULD I NOT SWIM, THEN, AS WELL AS A DUCK?"

"SAW THE LEAVES OF GOLD"

The Little Pine Tree

Far down in the forest, where the warm sun and the fresh air made a sweet resting place, grew a little pine tree. It had needles that were green all the year round, and yet it was not happy.

"I do not like needles," said the little tree; "they are not even so pretty as leaves. I should like to be the most lovely tree in the forest. I wish I had golden leaves." And lo! when the morning came, it found that its wish had been granted. It had leaves of gold that shone in the sunlight. How happy it was!

After a while a man, walking through the forest, saw the leaves of gold, and cried: "I'll be rich to-day!" He ran at once to the tree, and began to pluck the leaves, so that when he went away the little tree was quite bare, and was as vexed as a tree could be.

"I see it is not well to have gold leaves," said the little pine. "They are very pretty, but I should like something that people would not take from me. I wish I had leaves of glass. They would be pretty, and yet no one would want to take them."

The next morning, when the little tree awoke, it was covered with leaves of glass, that shone brightly in the sunlight. "Now, am I not gay?" it said. But presently the wind began to blow, and the glass leaves were dashed against one another. Soon they were all broken to pieces. When night came, the little tree was again without a leaf.

"Leaves of gold and glass are pretty," it said, "but they

are not the best. I should like to have green leaves like other trees." The next morning, when the little tree awoke, it had green leaves like other trees, and, "After all," it said, "green leaves are best. Now I am like the other trees, only even more lovely." But after a while a hungry goat came by, and the leaves of the little tree were fresh and sweet, so that he soon ate them all.

That night the little tree was again without a leaf. It was very sad, and said: "Gold leaves are fine, glass leaves are pretty, and green leaves are good for other trees; but, after all, I think my needles were best for me. How I wish I could have them back again!"

The next morning, when the little tree awoke, it had its needles once again.

MORAL.—*The thing you are is always the thing that you had better be.*

A Wolf turned Shepherd

A Swallow and a Spider

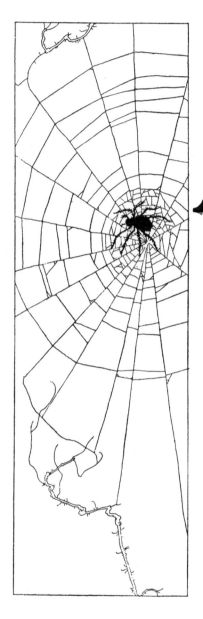

𝔄 𝔖wallow and a 𝔖pider

A SPIDER that observed a swallow catching flies fell immediately to work upon a net to catch swallows, for she looked upon it as an encroachment upon her right. But the birds, without any difficulty, broke through her work, and flew away with the very net itself.

"Well," says the spider, "bird-catching is not one of my talents I perceive," and so she returned to her old trade of catching flies again.

MORAL.—*It is well to learn by experience.*

"CALLED A COMPANY OF LITTLE BIRDS TOGETHER"

A Swallow and Other Birds

There was a country fellow at work sowing flax seeds, and a swallow (being a bird famous for providence and foresight) called a company of little birds about her, and bade them take good notice what the man was doing.

"You must know," says the swallow, "that all the fowler's nets or snares are made of hemp, or flax; and that's the seed that he is now sowing. Pick it up in time, for fear of what may come of it."

But despite the swallow's advice the other birds put it off, till it took root; and then again, till it was sprung up into the blade. Upon this, the swallow told them, once for all, that it was not yet too late to prevent the mischief, if they would but bestir themselves, and set heartily about it. But finding that no heed was given to what she said, she bade adieu to her old companions in the woods, and betook herself to a city life, and the company of men. This flax came in time to be gathered, and wrought into hemp, and it was this swallow's fortune to see several of the very same birds that she had forewarned taken in nets made of the very stuff she told them of. They came at last to be sensible of the folly of slipping their opportunity, but not until after they were lost.

MORAL.—*Fools will not believe in the effects of causes until it is too late to prevent them.*

A Stag Drinking

AS a stag was drinking upon the bank of a clear stream, he saw his image in the water, and entered upon this contemplation upon it:

"Well," says he, "if these pitiful legs of mine were but answerable to this branching head, I can but think how I should defy all my enemies!"

The words were hardly out of his mouth, when he discovered a pack of dogs coming full cry towards him. Away he scours across the fields, casts off the dogs, and gains a wood; but pressing through a thicket, the bushes held him by the horns, till the hounds came in and plucked him down. The last thing he said was:

"What an unhappy fool was I, to take my friends for my enemies, and my enemies for my friends! I trusted to my head, that has betrayed me, and I found fault with my legs, that would otherwise have brought me off safely."

MORAL.—*Handsome is as handsome does.*

156

"A STAG WAS DRINKING UPON THE BANK OF A CLEAR STREAM"

157

𝕬 𝕸erchant and a 𝕾eaman

MERCHANT at sea was asking the ship's master what death his father died. He told him that his father, his grandfather, and his great-grandfather were all drowned.

"Well," says the merchant, "and are not you yourself afraid of being drowned, too?"

"No, not I," says the skipper. "But pray," adds he, "what death did your father, grandfather, and great-grandfather die?"

"Why, they died all in their beds," says the merchant.

"Very good," says the skipper, "and why should I be any more afraid of going to sea than you are of going to bed?"

MORAL.—*Do not judge the feelings of others by your own.*

THE MERCHANT AND THE SEAMAN

REYNARD LAUGHS AT THE GOAT

𝕬 𝕱𝖔𝖝 𝖆𝖓𝖉 𝖆 𝕲𝖔𝖆𝖙

A FOX and a goat went down by consent into a well to drink; and when they had quenched their thirst, the goat fell to hunting up and down which way to get back again.

"Oh," says Reynard, "never trouble your head how to get back, but leave that to me! Do you but raise yourself upon your hinder legs with your forefeet close to the wall, and then stretch out your head. I can easily whip up to your horns, and so out of the well, and draw you after me."

The goat puts himself in a posture immediately, as he was directed, gives the fox a lift, and so out he springs; but Reynard's business was only to make sport with his companion, instead of helping him. Some hard words the goat gave him, but the fox puts off all with a jest.

"If you had but half so much brain as beard," says he, "you would have bethought yourself how to get up again before you went down."

MORAL.—*A wise man should consider well before resolving upon any serious action.*

An Oak and a Willow

THERE happened a controversy between an oak and a willow upon the subject of strength, constancy, and patience, and which of the two should have the preference. The oak upbraided the willow, that it was weak and wavering, and gave way to every blast. The willow made no other reply than that the next tempest should resolve that question. Some very little while after this dispute there came a violent storm. The willow bent and gave way to the gust, and still recovered itself again without receiving any damage; but the oak was stubborn, and chose rather to break than bend.

MORAL.—*A wise and steady man bends only with the prospect of rising again.*

The Fox and the Turkeys

Against a robber fox, a tree
    Some turkeys served as citadel.
That villain, much provoked to see
    Each standing there as sentinel,
      Cried out: "Such witless birds
At me stretch out their necks, and gobble!
No, by the powers, I'll give them trouble!"
    He verified his words.

163

THE FOX AND THE TURKEYS

The moon, that shone full on the oak,
Seem'd then to help the turkey folk.
But fox, in arts of siege well versed,
Ransack'd his bag of tricks accursed.
He feign'd himself about to climb;
Walk'd on his hinder legs sublime;
Then death most aptly counterfeited,
And seem'd anon resuscitated.
A practiser of wizard arts
Could not have fill'd so many parts.
In moonlight he contrived to raise
His tail, and make it seem a blaze:
And countless other tricks like that.
Meanwhile, no turkey slept or sat.
Their constant vigilance at length,
As hoped the fox, wore out their strength.
Bewilder'd by the rigs he run,
They lost their balance one by one.
As Reynard slew, he laid aside,
Till nearly half of them had died;
Then proudly to his larder bore,
And laid them up, an ample store.

MORAL.—

A foe, by being over-heeded,
Has often in his plan succeeded.

The Beasts and a Boot

In a dark wood, where wild beasts lived, there once lay a man's boot. How it came there it would be difficult to say. No man had been there; at least the wild beasts had not seen one in all their lives. But there the boot lay, and when the beasts saw it they all came round to talk about it. Though they had never seen such a thing before, they were all quite sure that they knew what it was.

"Why, there is no doubt at all, I say," said the bear. "Of course it is the rind of some kind of fruit—the fruit of the cork, I fancy. This is cork, it is plain to see," and he showed the sole of the boot.

"It's not that at all," said the wolf. "Of course it is some kind of nest. Look! here is the hole for the bird to go in, and here is the deep part where the eggs and young ones may be safe. No doubt at all, of course not!"

"It is not that at all," said the goat. "How can you be so silly! Look at this long root!" and he pointed to the bootlace: "it is the root of the plant, of course." Thus

165

they went on talking, until by and by they began to get angry with one another.

"If I might speak," said an old owl, who had been sitting silent in a tree near, "I think I could tell you what it is. I have been in a land where there are more of such things than you could count. It is a man's boot."

"A what?" cried all the beasts and birds. "What is a man, and what is a boot?"

"A man," said the owl, "is a thing with two legs but no feathers. He can walk, and eat, and talk like us; but he can do more than we can."

"That can't be true," said the beasts. "How can a thing with two legs do more than we can, who have four? It is false, of course." "Of course it is, if they have no wings," added the birds.

"Well," went on the owl, "they have no wings, and yet it is true. And they can make things like this. They call them boots, and put them on their feet."

"Not true! not true!" they all cried. "We know that such things are not worn on the feet. How could they be? You have said what you know is false. You are not fit to live with us. You must leave the wood." They chased the poor old owl out of the wood, and would not let him come back.

"It is true for all that," said the owl; and of course it was.

MORAL.—*It is foolish to say that is untrue which does not happen to have come within our own experience.*

"THEY CHASED THE POOR OLD OWL OUT OF THE WOOD"

An Ass and a Lion

IN old times a lion shook hands with an ass, and they agreed to jog on up and down in the woods, lovingly and peaceably together. As they were upon this adventure they discovered a pack of wolves. The ass immediately set up a hideous bray, and ran at them open mouthed, as if he would have eaten them. The wolves only sneered at him for his pains, but scampered away, however, as hard as they could drive. By and by the ass comes back again, puffing and blowing, from the chase.

"Well," says the lion, "and what was that horrid scream for, I prithee?"

"Why," says the other, "I frightened them all away, you see."

"And did they run away from you," says the lion, "or from me, do you think?"

MORAL.—*Vanity thinks itself important when it is only laughable.*

A Swallow and Other Birds

An Oak and a Willow

"IN OLD TIMES A LION SHOOK HANDS WITH AN ASS"

A Snake and a File

There once was a snake that, having got into a smith's shop, fell to licking a file. After a time she saw that on the file there was blood, and the more blood appeared on it the more eagerly she licked, having a foolish fancy that it was the file that bled, and that she felt the better for it.

At the conclusion, when she could lick no longer, she fell to biting; but finding at last she could do no more upon it with her teeth than with her tongue, she fairly left it.

MORAL.—*In seeking to hurt another we frequently only wound ourselves.*

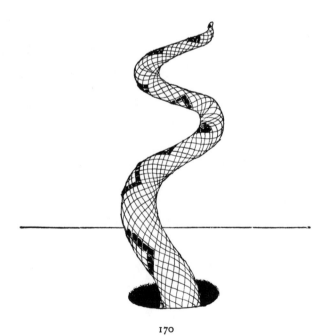

A BEE AND THE DRONES

A Bee that went over to the Drones

"To what end," says a bee, "should I toil and moil myself out of my life for a poor subsistence, when the drones that do nothing at all live in as much plenty every jot as I do?" Upon this thought the bee resolved after their example to work no longer.

The master, it seems, called her to account for it; the bee was offended, and, without any more to-do, went over to the drones' party, where she passed the summer easily enough, and to her satisfaction. But upon winter's coming on, when the drones were all dispersed into their several holes, the bee would fain have gone home again; but the cells of the combs were all closed, so that there was no entrance, and the poor bee starved to death betwixt cold and hunger.

MORAL.—*That nobody has a right to be idle.*

The Brier and the Gardener

Says the brier, one day, to the gardener:

"Hark ye, honest John; what is it I have done to you that you should use me after this manner? Do you think now that I am in my right place? What is the matter that I must not have the same respect and treatment as the other fruit trees? On my conscience, John, you don't use me with common civility.

"Why, now, what signifies it for me to stand staring up in a hedge, as if I had nothing else to do but to be a porter to your enclosure? No, no, prithee put me into your garden; for I have as good blood in my veins as any plant of them all, though they hold their noses so high. Do as I bid you, if you have any regard to the interest of yourself and family. You'll never know what advantage it will be to you. Only try for once, and, I promise you, you'll gain by it.

"Besides, I require the least attendance of any plant alive. Why, man, thou hast nothing to do but to water me now and then, and cover me a little from the north wind or so, and I'll engage to reward your care with fruits of the most excellent and delicious flavour; and then, for flowers, your roses and lilies must not pretend to go beyond me. I could say a great deal more, if modesty would permit me, but I hate to praise myself; only make the experiment, and I am well satisfied in a little time you'll come and tell me that my words bear no proportion with my actions."

"HARK YE, HONEST JOHN"

173

In these terms the pride and self-love of a useless plant were expressed, and poor John was so silly as to give entire credit to every syllable; for you must understand in those times, when plants could speak, gardeners were not so cunning as they are now.

Well, the brier was transplanted, and spread out against a wall, and watered three or four times a day at least, for John was big with expectation of mighty things, and therefore could not trust to the dew. In short, the favourite brier was the gardener's only care; and, indeed, she was as good as her word, for she grew to a miracle, spreading wide her root and branches.

But, alas! these prickly branches were destruction to the neighbouring plants; everything within their reach withered away, fruits and pot herbs expired, and the gayest flowers drooped, and hung down their heads and died. Poor John was then convinced of his folly, and would never afterwards give credit to any plant whatsoever on its own bare word.

MORAL.—*Everything that a boaster says should not be believed.*

The Tortoise and the Two Ducks

A light-brain'd tortoise, anciently,
Tired of her hole, the world would see.
Prone are all such, self-banish'd, to roam—
Prone are. all cripples to abhor their home.
  Two ducks, to whom the gossip told
  The secret of her purpose bold,
    Profess'd to have the means whereby
    They could her wishes gratify.
  "Our boundless road," said they, "behold!
    It is the open air;
    And through it we will bear
  You safe o'er land and ocean.
Republics, kingdoms, you will view,
And famous cities, old and new;
    And get of customs, laws, a notion—
Of various wisdom various pieces,
As did, indeed the safe Ulysses."

"IT MADE THE PEOPLE GAPE AND STARE"

THE TWO DUCKS

The eager tortoise waited not
To question what Ulysses got,
But closed the bargain on the spot.
A nice machine the birds devise
To bear their pilgrim through the skies.
Athwart her mouth a stick they throw.
"Now bite it hard, and don't let go,"
They say, and seize each duck an end,
And, swiftly flying, upward tend.
It made the people gape and stare
  Beyond the expressive power of words,
To see a tortoise cut the air,
  Exactly poised between two birds.
"A miracle," they cried, "is seen!
There goes the flying tortoise queen!"
"The queen!" ('t was thus the tortoise spoke);
"I'm truly that, without a joke."
Much better had she held her tongue
For, opening that whereby she clung,
Before the gazing crowd she fell,
And dashed to bits her brittle shell.

MORAL.—

Imprudence, vanity, and babble,
  And idle curiosity,
An ever-undivided rabble,
  Have all the same paternity.

𝔄 Jackdaw and Borrowed Feathers

A jackdaw, that had a mind to appear grand, tricked himself up with all the gay feathers he could muster together; and upon the credit of these stolen or borrowed ornaments valued himself above all the birds in the air beside. The pride of this vanity got him the envy of all his companions, who, upon a discovery of the truth of the case, fell to plucking him by consent; and when every bird had taken his own feather the silly jackdaw had nothing left him to cover his nakedness.

MORAL.—*It is foolish to take pride in borrowed plumes.*

178

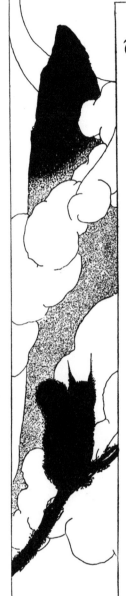

The Mountain and the Squirrel

The mountain and the squirrel
    Had a quarrel,
And the former called the latter
    "Little Prig";
    Bun replied:
"You are doubtless very big;
But all sorts of things and weather
Must be taken in together
To make up a year,
And a sphere.
And I think it no disgrace
To occupy my place.
If I'm not so large as you,
You are not so small as I,
And not half so spry.
I'll not deny you make
A very pretty squirrel track;
Talents differ; all is well and wisely
    put;
If I cannot carry forests on my back,
Neither can you crack a nut."

MORAL.—*Each man should do that
work for which he is fitted.*

THE RIVAL SCULPTORS

180

The Two Statues

IN a certain great city in old times, the people were resolved to set up the statue of Pallas upon the top of a magnificent temple. To this great work the whole city contributed, and the two Phidiases were pitched upon to make each of them one, and he that made the best was to have the price, which was no small one. The people were to judge. One only was to have the money, and consequently the honour, and the other nothing.

Well, to work they went with all possible expedition, and the hopes of gain and reputation had so fired our two artists, that in a little time their work was finished and brought to the porch of the temple. The whole town ran thither, and judgment was soon given for one of them, and the other treated with contempt. Well, this was a beautiful piece; it had a thousand graces: how soft and delicate were the lines and features, the limbs round and lively; nothing could possibly come up to it; criticism itself could find no fault with it.

The other statue was nothing but a rough, shapeless piece of marble, nothing finished, the features big and ugly, the limbs monstrous, and shape frightful. Well, we must send this back again, that's certain; this man is only a learner, we see, a mere novice, the other a perfect master, and he must have the money.

They were going to give it him, when the despised sculptor steps up. "Hold, gentlemen," says he, "this must be tried. Do you think I made my statue for the porch? Let them both be put on the top of the temple, as they were intended, and then you'll see which is most perfect."

This was done, though with a great deal of grumbling at the unnecessary expense. But, alas! how things were then changed! The statue so much before admired lost all its charms; they entirely vanished at such a distance, which gave the other all those beauties no one imagined it could have when they surveyed it near.

MORAL.—*We must look at everything in its proper place.*

An Eagle sets up for a Beauty

It was once put to the question among the birds which of the whole tribe of them was the greatest beauty. The eagle gave her voice for herself, and carried it.

"Yes," says a peacock in a soft voice, "you are a great beauty indeed, but it lies in your beak and in your talons, that make it death to dispute it."

MORAL.—*Homage is more often paid by fear than by love.*

"THE EAGLE GAVE HER VOICE FOR HERSELF"

THE THRUSH AND THE JAY
184

The Thrush and the Jay

The Ant and the Cricket

The Thrush and the Jay

"When shall you build your nest?" said a thrush to a jay one fine day in spring.

"Oh, by and by!" said the jay. "It is so fine now, I must hop, and fly, and sing, and have fun while I can."

"One can sing while one works," said the thrush; "there is surely no need to stop work for that."

"When shall *you* build your nest?" asked the jay.

"Mine! Oh, I have built some of it! Look!" And the thrush, with a glad chirp, showed the bush where she had laid moss, and twigs, and twined them so as to make a nest. "And now," said she, "I must be off to get some hay, or wool, or some more moss to go on with."

"Oh, come and have a bit of play!" said the jay. "Why don't you rest a bit."

"Oh, that will come by and by!" said the thrush. And she sang her song:

> "When I 've done, I 'll have my fun;
> Then in my nest I 'll take my rest;
> That I know will be the best."

"Well, well," said the jay, "if you like to slave the best part of your life, pray do."

"Of course," said the thrush; "the best part of my life is the time for work."

"There will be time for work by and by," said the jay."

"There will be time for play and rest by and by," said the thrush. And off she flew and sang her short, gay song.

"I don't like that song," said the jay.

Day by day it was just the same. The thrush had built her nest, and laid five eggs in it, and yet the jay had not brought one stick to make hers. At last, in great haste, she got some twigs and grass and laid them on a branch in a high tree. But she did not place them well, and when she had worked for an hour or two, she left off, and went to see the thrush, who sat on a bush close by.

"When will your nest be done?" said the thrush.

"Oh, by and by!" said the jay. "I must rest now. Have you found time to rest yet?"

"Oh dear no!" said the thrush. "Just look. I have five dear little ones here. How could I leave them or find time to play? I bring them food, or else sit here to keep them warm all day and all night."

"How dull you must be!" said the jay.

"Not at all," said the thrush; "they are such dear, sweet, little things. But I must be off to get them some food," and away she flew.

The jay's nest was not done when one day she saw the thrush with all her young ones on the soft grass.

"Have you built your nest yet?" cried the thrush.

"No," said the jay. "At least it is not done yet. But I have laid my eggs, and the rest of the nest I can build by and by, when they are hatched."

"That will not do," thought the thrush, but she did not say so. That night came a great storm. It rocked the tree where the jay had laid her eggs on the loose twigs and grass, and one by one they slipped from the nest and fell to the ground. When the jay woke next day, all her eggs were gone, and bits of shell lay on the ground at the foot of the tree. And that was what came of the jay's "by and by". But the thrush and her five young ones, all safe and well, had time for rest, and also for play.

MORAL.—*There is a proper time for work and a proper time for play.*

A Satyr and Fire

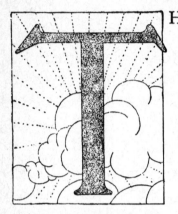THE poets tell us that Prometheus stole some of Jupiter's fire, and brought it down to us from heaven, and that was our original of it. A satyr was so transported with the glory and splendour of this spirit that down on his knees he falls, and would needs kiss and embrace it.

"Have a care of your beard," says Prometheus; "nay, and of your chin too; for it will both singe and burn you."

"And why," says the satyr, "would you bring down so glorious a temptation then to plague the world withal?"

"Why," says Prometheus, "there were no living without it, only the mischief lies in the abuse. It burns, 'tis true, but then consider the heat and the light that come along with it, and you shall find it serves us to all manner of profitable, delightful, and necessary purposes, provided only that we make a right use of it."

MORAL.—*That which is good for use may be made bad by abuse.*

"'HAVE A CARE OF YOUR BEARD,' SAYS PROMETHEUS"

The Ant and the Cricket

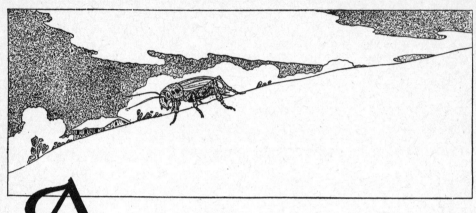

A SILLY young cricket, accustomed to sing
Through the warm sunny months of the
summer and spring,
Began to complain when he found that at home
His cupboard was empty and winter was come.
  Not a crumb to be found
  On the snow-covered ground;
  Not a flower could he see,
  Nor a leaf on a tree;
"Oh, what will become," said the cricket, "of me?"

At last, by starvation and famine made bold,
All dripping with wet and trembling with cold,
Away he set off to a hardworking ant
To see if, to keep him alive, he would grant
  A shelter from rain
  And a mouthful of grain;
  He wished only to borrow
  And repay it to-morrow.
If not, he must die of starvation and sorrow.

"AWAY HE SET OFF TO A HARDWORKING ANT"

Said the ant to the cricket: "I'm your servant and
    friend;
But we ants never borrow, we ants never lend.
But tell me, dear sir, did you lay nothing by
When the weather was warm?" Said the cricket:
      "Not I."
    My heart was so light
    That I sang day and night;
    For all nature was gay."
    "You sang, sir, you say?
Go then," said the ant, "and dance winter away.

MORAL.—*There is one time for work and another time for play*

A Boy and False Alarms

A SHEPHERD'S boy had a roguish trick of crying "A wolf! a wolf!" when there was no such animal about, and fooling the country people with false alarms. He had been at this sport so many times in jest, that they would not believe him at last when he was in earnest; and so the wolves brake in upon the flock, and worried the sheep at their pleasure.

MORAL.—*It is foolish to jest about serious things.*

The Crab and its Mother

" Don't walk aslant, nor o'er the moist rock draw
Crosswise," its dam said to the crab, " thy claw."
" Nay, first," cried he, " Mother and mentor too,
" Walk straight yourself; I 'll watch and follow you."

MORAL.—*Example is better than precept.*

The Ploughshare and the Sword

Once upon a time, a great many years since, the plough-share and the sword met one another in the fields. The sword, it seems, being a person of quality, had his head so full of nobility, that he would hardly look at anyone beneath his rank.

The ploughshare saluted him after his way, and made a bow, but the sword took no manner of notice.

"Pray, good sir," says he, "whence comes this stately carriage?"

"And don't you know?" says the sword; "a very pretty question truly. Why, you are a country bumpkin, and I of quality, that's all."

"Aye, say you so," says the ploughshare; "and how, in the name of goodness, did you come by your gentility? You do nothing but mischief, while my whole being is employed in doing good to the world; my labour and industry is the support of mankind; they can't live without me. You take away lives by dozens, and very often for nothing at all."

"Poor creeping thing," says the sword, "what a mean soul hast thou! And dost think great men are of thy silly opinion?"

"Yes, indeed," replies the ploughshare; "we have seen mighty conquerors retire, and lay their triumphant hands again to the plough. Witness the Romans, our lords and masters."

"But dost thou think, blockhead, that these Romans could, without my help, have subdued the world. Rome had been only a small village, and no one would have talked of her, if my power had not made mankind her slaves."

"So much the worse," says the ploughshare. "She had much better have been quiet. A very fine necessity, truly, that the whole world should become slaves to one town, which by her prodigious cruelties frightened all Europe, Africa, and Asia into subjection! And why, for what end, good your honour? Only to please a restless ambition which is never satisfied. And do you think this deserves such commendation?"

The sword was now at the end of his logic, and, very much like a gentleman, challenged Gaffer Ploughshare.

"Come," says he, "let us fight it out, for I'll have satisfaction."

"That's your trade," says the ploughshare, "but it is not mine. I am one of the rude country bumpkins, as your honour is pleased to call me, who never practised the gentleman-like way of cutting one another's throats for trifles. I work, sir, and never fight. But I tell you what I'll do with you; let a third person decide the controversy. Let us choose the mole for our arbitrator. She is like Themis, she has no eyes, has a very grave air, and wears a black furred gown; you cannot choose better." This was agreed upon, and each told his story.

Our new Themis heard all distinctly in her hole, and, having very judiciously weighed all circumstances, pronounced sentence in this proverb: He that forged the ploughshare was a wise man, but he that made the sword was a fool.

Moral.—*It is better to cultivate than to destroy.*

"THE PLOUGHSHARE AND THE SWORD MET ONE ANOTHER"

𝕬 𝕱𝖔𝖝 𝖆𝖓𝖉 𝖆 𝕮𝖆𝖙

There was a question started betwixt a fox and a cat, which of the two could make the best shift in the world if put to a pinch.

"For my own part," says Reynard, "when the worst comes to the worst, I have a number of tricks to save myself with at last."

At that very instant up comes a pack of dogs full cry towards them. The cat presently takes a tree, and sees the poor fox torn to pieces upon the very spot.

MORAL.—*One sure trick is better than a hundred slippery ones.*

"THE CAT PRESENTLY TAKES A TREE"

The Heifer, Goat, and Sheep in Company with the Lion

The heifer, the goat, and their sister the sheep
Compacted their earnings in common to keep,
'T is said, in time past, with a lion, who sway'd
Full lordship o'er neighbours, of whatever grade.
The goat, as it happen'd, a stag having snared,
Sent off to the rest, that the beast might be shared.
All gather'd; the lion first counts on his claws,
And says: "We'll proceed to divide with our paws
The stag into pieces, as fix'd by our laws."
This done, he announces part first as his own.
"'T is mine," he says, "truly, as lion alone."
To such a decision there's naught to be said,
As he who has made it is doubtless the head.
"Well, also, the second to me should belong;
'T is mine, be it known, by the right of the strong.
Again, as the bravest, the third must be mine.
To touch but the fourth whoso maketh a sign,
        I 'll choke him to death
        In the space of a breath!"

MORAL.—*Those who go into partnership with a lion must
    expect him to take the lion's share.*

200

The Crab and its Mother

A Mountain and a Mouse

The Phoenix chosen King

The government of the birds was in olden times an elective monarchy, and there happened once a notable debate among their representatives about the choice of a new king. They put upon the first place the eagles, vultures, goshawks, falcons, and, in short, all the birds of prey; for a prince, they cried, must be martial, strong, and resolute, else he can never govern as he should. It was then objected, on the other side, that no true lover of his country's liberty would give his vote for a ruler that lived upon rapine and the very heart's blood of his people. This single stroke quite dashed the first motion.

The next that pretended were the ostriches, the jays, the peacocks, and other birds that value themselves upon a sparkish outside, and the beauty of their plumes. But kings, they said, were not for show, but business, and it was not the feather in the cap but the brains in the head of a man that qualified him for government; so that the second candidates succeeded no better than the former.

There came on in the third place the parrots and the starlings, and the rest of that fantastical crew, that value themselves upon the faculty of excellent ready speakers; but they were answered with the sentence of the wise man: In many words there is much folly. And it was then resolved upon the question, that to have the tongue run before the wit is the quality of a buffoon, not of a governor; so that these blades came off not one jot better than their fellows.

The fourth that stood in nomination was the crow, a bird in high reputation for wisdom, experience, and fore-sight. His friends in the council stuck so close to him that he was within a hairbreadth of carrying it; but yet after a long discussion the vote passed against him. His very adversaries could not in truth deny him to be so qualified as his friends rendered him; but then his wisdom, they said, was a wisdom of interest, and a sagacity that only led him to his prey and to the gratifying of a depraved appetite; for carrion was his daily food: but it was unlucky still, and ill-boding.

With that, up stood an eminent member at the Board and moved for the Phœnix. "If you'll have a king," says he, "beyond expression—a king to your very wish and liking—apply yourselves to the Phœnix, a creature, that for a generous bravery of mind, a gracious person, a charming elocution, a consummate wisdom and insight into the darkest secrets and intrigues of reason or state, is as much beyond all the rest of the competitors as an angelical perfection is beyond the common frailties of flesh and blood. He has neither wife nor children to divert him from attending to his charge; no passions to transport him; but you may live easily under him, without the burden either of laws or taxes."

As the member was going on, the assembly interrupted him in the middle of his harangue, crying out unanimously: "A Phœnix! a Phœnix!" and couriers were immediately dispatched away through all quarters of the earth to try to find him out, and to give him an invitation, in the name of the freeborn subjects of the woods, to take possession of his new government. In one word, when they had

"COURIERS WERE IMMEDIATELY DISPATCHED"

"UP STANDS ONE OF THE COMPANY WITH A CHALLENGE"

searched every corner of the world without getting any tidings of him, they came back again just as wise as they set out.

MORAL.—*There is nothing perfect under the sun, and if nothing imperfect will satisfy us we must never be satisfied.*

A Silly Fop

As a number of gambolling young fellows were together trying feats of activity, up stands one of the company with a challenge.

"Look ye, my masters," says he; "you shall see me stand upon one leg now, a whole hour together, and I defy any man of the club to do it after me."

"Nay," says one of the gang, "there's none of this company will pretend to it, sure, but I'll show you a goose that can."

MORAL.—*He that prides himself upon the faculties of a goose is likely to live and die a goose.*

The Sheep Leagued against the Wolves

A shepherd found his flock so infested with wolves that he called his sheep together, and reasoned the matter with them in a formal speech:

"You are a great number," says he, "and your heads are armed; the wolves not near so many, and they have no horns; so that if you would but pluck up your hearts, and stand upon your guards, they would not dare to meddle with you."

The sheep were then one and all for putting it to a push; but when the first wolf appeared, they were one and all again for betaking themselves to their heels.

MORAL.—*Sheep will be sheep.*

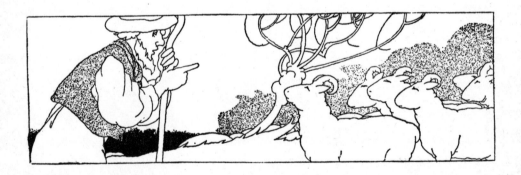

THE SHEEP RUN AWAY ON THE APPEARANCE OF THE WOLF

207

A Wolf, Kid, and Goat

GOAT that was going out one morning for a mouthful of fresh grass, charged her kid not to open the door, till she came back, to any creature that had not a beard. The goat was no sooner out of sight but up comes a wolf to the door, that had overheard the charge, and in a small pipe calls to the kid to let her mother come in. The kid smelt the roguery, and bade the wolf show his beard, and the door should be open to him.

MORAL.—*However a hypocrite may be disguised, there is always some mark by which he may be known.*

"UP COMES A WOLF TO THE DOOR"

"AND THAT WHICH EASED THE ONE DROWNED THE OTHER"

Two Laden Asses

As two asses were fording a river, the one laden with salt, the other with sponge, the salt ass fell down under his burden, but quickly got up again, and went on the merrier for it. The sponge ass found it agreed so well with his companion that down lies he too, upon the same experiment; but the water that dissolved the salt made the sponge forty times heavier than it was before, and that which eased the one drowned the other.

MORAL.—*That which is good in one case may be bad in another.*

𝕿𝖍𝖊 𝕮𝖍𝖆𝖒𝖊𝖑𝖊𝖔𝖓

Two of those sort of gentlemen who would see everything, though they travelled all over the world, who for the sake of saying: "I have seen it and ought to know it," have (if you'll believe them) traversed the whole globe; in short, two travellers (no matter for their names) were once upon a time trotting on in the plains of Africa, and discoursing of the nature of the chameleon.

"A wonderful creature, this chameleon," says one of them, "and very particular! I never saw the like in my life; his head shaped like a fish, his little body perfect lizard, with his long tail, his four little paws with three fingers, his motion so slow, he can scarce travel a foot in a month's time, and, above all, his colour deep mazarine blue and——"

"Hold there, I beseech you. I must here beg your pardon indeed, sir, for it is a beautiful green. I have seen him with these two eyes of mine very plain, and as long as I pleased. He was then basking in the sun with his mouth wide open, sucking in the pure air for his dinner."

"Don't be angry," replied the other; "he is blue. I observed him at better advantage than you did, for he was then in the shade."

"He is green, I say."

"Blue, I tell you."

"You lie!"

And so they went at it, when there came by a third.

"Hey day, gentlemen!" says he; "what, are you both mad? Stop a little, and let me know the cause of this difference."

"With all my soul," says one of the combatants, "and be you judge of the quarrel. Our dispute was about the chameleon, and what colour he was. Monsieur here says he is green, and I say he is blue. Now, pray, sir——"

"Agree, agree," says our grave judge, "for to tell you the truth he is neither; he is coal black. Last night, I am sure, I examined him very carefully, and here I have him in my handkerchief."

"No, no, that is impossible," says one of the contenders; "he is green, I'll give you my word and honour."

"He is blue," says the other, "and I'll lay my life on't."

"Gentlemen, are you not a couple of silly fellows, when I know he is black; and to confute you both, look here," and he opened his handkerchief, and the poor creature, to the astonishment of both judge and parties, appeared as white as snow.

"Get you about your business, "says the chameleon, "like three childish creatures as you are. You are all right, and all in the wrong. Believe henceforward there are eyes as good as your own. Speak your own sentiments, but don't be such fools as to imagine you can make every man's judgment submit to yours."

MORAL—*Do not insist upon others being wrong because you believe yourself to be right.*

𝔄 𝔐𝔬𝔲𝔫𝔱𝔞𝔦𝔫 𝔞𝔫𝔡 𝔞 𝔐𝔬𝔲𝔰𝔢

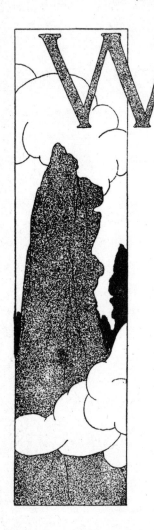

WHEN mountains cry out, people may well be excused the fear of some prodigious birth. This was the case in the fable. The neighbourhood were all at their wits' end to consider what would come forth after the roaring of the mountain; when, instead of the dreadful monster that they expected, out came at last a ridiculous mouse.

MORAL.—*There is often much ado about nothing.*

"OUT CAME AT LAST A RIDICULOUS MOUSE"

215

"WOULD HAVE STOPPED HIS BARKING BY GIVING HIM FOOD"

A Dog and a Thief

As a gang of thieves were at work to rob a house, a mastiff took the alarm, and fell a-baying. One of the company spoke to him, and would have stopped his barking by giving him food.

"No," says the dog, "this will not do, for several reasons. First, I'll take no bribes to betray my master. Secondly, I'm not such a fool as to sell the ease and liberty of my whole life to come, for a piece of bread in hand; for when you have rifled my master, pray who shall maintain me?"

MORAL.—*Fair words and flattery are sometimes the tools of treason.*

The Pig and the Hen

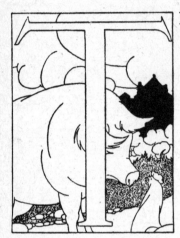

THE pig and the hen,
Both got in one pen,
And the hen said she wouldn't go
out.
"Mistress Hen," says the pig,
"Don't you be quite so big!"
And he gave her a push with his
snout.

"You are rough and you're fat,
But who cares for all that:
I will stay if I choose," says the hen.
"No, mistress no longer!"
Says pig: "I'm the stronger;
And master I'll be of my pen!"

Then the hen cackled out
Just as close to his snout
As she dare: "You're an ill-natured pig;
And if I had the corn,
Just as sure as I'm born,
I would send you to starve or to dig!"

"But you don't own the cribs;
So I think that my ribs

THE HEN

"THE PIG AND THE HEN, BOTH GOT IN ONE PEN"

Will be never the leaner for you.
  This trough is my trough,
  And the sooner you 're off,"
Says the pig, "why, the better you 'll do!"

"You 're not a bit fair,
And you 're cross as a bear.
What harm do I do in your pen?
  But a pig is a pig,
  And I don't care a fig
For the worst you can say," says the hen.

Says the pig, "You will care
If I act like a bear,
And tear your two wings from your neck."
  "What a nice little pen
  You have got!" says the hen,
Beginning to scratch and to peck.

Now the pig stood amazed,
And the bristles upraised
A moment past, fell down so sleek,
  "Neighbour Biddy," says he,
  "If you 'll just allow me,
I will show you a nice place to pick."

So she followed him off,
And they ate from one trough—

THE HEN

They had quarrelled for nothing, they saw;
  And when they had fed,
   "Neighbour Hen," the pig said,
"Won't you stay here and roost in my straw?"

"No, I thank you; you see
That I sleep in a tree,"
Says the hen; "but I must go away;
  So a grateful goodbye."
  "Make your home in my sty,"
Says the pig, "and come in every day."

MORAL.—

Now my child will not miss
The true meaning of this
Little story of anger and strife;
  For a word spoken soft
  Will turn enemies oft
Into friends—that will stay friends for life.

An Eagle and other Birds

A company of birds were chattering together in a congregation, every one of them setting up for itself, and its own kind, some in one way, and some in another. The hawk valued herself upon a rank wing; the crow, upon her skill in augury; the nightingale, upon her delicate singing; the peacock, upon its beauty; the partridge, upon its craft; the wren, upon his mettle; the duck, upon her faculty in paddling; and the heron, upon the credit of being reputed weatherwise.

"Well!" says the eagle; "and what is all this now to a sharp, piercing eye, which, without vanity, is my talent in perfection. Or if any one of you make a doubt on't, let me but carry him up into the air and he shall see the experiment."

The wren, upon this, mounts the eagle, and the eagle, with the wren upon her back, works herself up to her pitch; and when she was now at lessening, she called to the wren to look down and tell her what she saw below?

"Alas," says the wren, "I have much ado to discern the very earth, at this distance!"

"But yet at the same time," says the eagle, "do I see a black sheep yonder without a tail, and you shall see me immediately make a stoop at it, and seize it."

And what was this black sheep at last, but a fowler's bait for some bird of prey. The eagle pushed at it, and fell into the snare herself.

"Ah!" says the wren; "if you had been but as quick-sighted to discover the danger, as you were to spy out the quarry, you would much more easily have found out the man with his birding-tackle, on the one side, than the sheep without a tail, on the other."

MORAL.—*Even the keenest sighted may be caught in a trap.*

The Eclipse

THE sun was one day travelling over the azure plains of heaven in his glittering car, preceded by the Hours. His radiant glories pierced through the regions of the air, and from the high realms of Olympus displayed the finest day that ever the world beheld.

The earth grew more beautiful, fertile, and luxuriant; Flora shone in every climate in her embroidery and tissue, and Ceres, with her golden tresses, displayed her treasures in the scattered plains. A thousand young suns sparkled in the water. In short, all nature smiled, and it seemed as if the whole world had a mind by her beauties to engage him to look on and admire her.

"Ah," says the moon, "this is too much! So much splendour offends my eyes. Does the sun pretend to have the sole dominion of heaven, and reign Lord Paramount there? I must destroy that pompous importunate lustre; so much glory is injurious to my person. I have a thought in my head, which when executed will teach the world what

I am.   It has ever belonged to us to make beautiful and pleasant nights; let us now, by right of conquest, show we can make fine days too.   The sun gives too much light; what I bestow is just enough."

What she had projected the silly fool put in execution, and went and placed herself between us and Phœbus, and gave him battle.   But, alas! what was the event of all this struggle? Did she shine more for that? No, on the contrary, this adventure, which spread a horrid darkness over the whole horizon, teaches us that my Lady Moon was only an obscure planet, and only borrowed her light from the sun her brother.

MORAL.—*It is well to make sure that you have light of your own before you try to make the world admire your shining.*

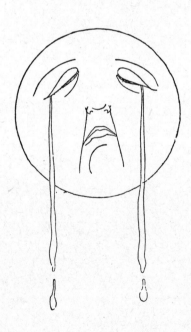

"WENT AND PLACED HERSELF BETWEEN US AND PHŒBUS"

A Father and his Sons

COUNTRYMAN that lived well in the world himself, upon the results of his honest labour and industry, was desirous that his sons should do so after him; and being upon his deathbed:

"My dear children," says he, "I reckon myself bound to tell you, before I depart, that there is a considerable treasure hid in my vineyard. Wherefore pray be sure to dig, and search narrowly for it when I am gone."

The father died, and the sons fell immediately to work upon the vineyard. They turned it up over and over, and not one penny of money to be found there—but the profit of the next vintage expounded the riddle.

MORAL.—*A good example and good counsel form the best legacy that a man can leave his children.*

"THEY TURNED IT UP OVER AND OVER"

"IN LION'S SKIN AN ASS ONCE WENT ABOUT"

228

The Ass wearing the Lion's Skin

In lion's skin an ass once went about,
And threw the brute creation into rout;
They thought him a true lion, not an ass.
He therefore tried, when Reynard chanced to pass,
If, like the rest, a fox would yield to fright.
But when he met that wily creature's sight
(Now she, by chance, that moment heard him bray),
Quoth she to him: "Be sure of what I say:
Had I not just now mark'd you when you bray'd,
I, like my fellow brutes, had been afraid."

MORAL.—*Even in a lion's skin an ass will betray that he is an ass.*

A Farmer and his Servant

A country farmer missed an ox out of his grounds, and sent his man abroad one day to look after him. The simpleton went hunting up and down, till at last he found him in a wood; but upon three birds coming near, away goes he scampering after them. He stayed so long upon the errand, that his master wondered what had become of him, and so abroad he goes to look for his man, and there was he in a field hard by, running as hard as he could drive, and staring up into the air.

"Well," says the master, "what news?"

"Why, master," says the man, "I have found them."

"Aye, but," says the farmer again, "where are they? And what have you found?"

"Why, look you, there they are," says the fellow. "I have found three birds here, and I'm trying if I can catch them."

MORAL.—*It is necessary to keep to the work in hand, and not go off after other things.*

The Ass, the Dog, and the Master

N ass, observing that his master was very kind to a little dog, who did him no service, but only leaped up and fawned upon him, and that nevertheless he spoke kindly to him, and made much of him, took him in his arms and stroked him, gave him many a good bit from his own table, while he, poor soul, worked hard, ate but little, and was beaten much, resolved to follow the dog's example, in hopes to fare for the future as well as he. The next time, therefore, that his master came near him, he leaped upon him, as he had often seen the dog do before. But the master, not wont to receive such rough salutation from his ass, and finding his weight something heavy, nor knowing how inno-

"LOADED HIM WITH HEAVIER BURDENS THAN BEFORE"

The Cat and the Mouse

A Fox and a Raven

cently the poor creature meant it, feared no less than that he intended to kill him. He therefore called his servants to his assistance, who, coming with cudgels in their hands, belaboured the ass full sore, and at length got him off. In short, they concluded, that too much ease had made him restive, and therefore they loaded him with heavier burdens than before, and at length sent him to the corn mill, where he ended his days in great shame and sorrow, the laughing-stock of the dogs and other asses.

MORAL.—*It is foolish to affect that which is unnatural.*

𝔄 𝔊𝔞𝔯𝔡𝔢𝔫𝔢𝔯 𝔞𝔫𝔡 𝔥𝔦𝔰 𝔏𝔞𝔫𝔡𝔩𝔬𝔯𝔡

A man who had made himself a very fine garden was so pestered with the damage done by a hare among his plants, that away went he immediately to his landlord, and told him a lamentable story of the havoc that this poor hare had made in his grounds. The gentleman takes pity of his tenant, and early the next morning goes over to him with all his people and his dogs about him. They call in the first place for breakfast, eat up his victuals, and drink him dry. So soon as they have done all the mischief they can within doors, out they march into the gardens to beat for the hare, and then—down with the hedges; the garden-stuff goes all to wreck, and not so much as a leaf that would go toward the picking of a salad escapes them.

"Well," says the gardener, "this is the way of the world, when the poor sue for relief from the great. My noble friend here has done me more damage in the civility and respect of these two hours than the uttermost spite of the hare could have done me in twice as many ages."

MORAL.—*It is sometimes dangerous for the weak to appeal for assistance to the strong.*

"THE GARDEN-STUFF GOES ALL TO WRECK"

"CAME SNIFFING ROUND"

236

The Cat and the Mouse

A gentle mouse happened one day to be decoyed into a trap, and lost her liberty for a bit of bacon. A cat, who had a delicate nose, came sniffing round, and viewed both bait and prisoner; and now all his wit was made use of to obtain these delicious morsels.

"Gossip," says he, in a whining, hypocritical tone, "let us lay aside all animosity. We have lived long enough at variance; I'm quite weary of it for my part. Now, if you are as sick of contention as I am, let us live in strict amity and friendship for the future; and I do assure you, though I say it that should not, you shall never know how much I am at your service."

"With all my heart," says the mouse.

"And you are in earnest?" says the cat.

"As I hope for mercy, am I," says the mouse, "and if I am not, may——"

"No imprecations, good madam, I beseech you," replied the cat. "But to ratify this treaty in all its forms, pray be so good as to open your lodging, that we may shake hands and embrace like sincere friends."

"I desire nothing more," says the mouse. "You have nothing else to do but to lift up that board at the entry, which is done by pulling down that long piece of wood there that sticks out like a barber's pole; that's all!"

The cat accordingly falls to work; and scarce had she set her two paws upon it, but up flew the trapdoor, and the mouse scampered away into her hole with the bacon, which she soon gobbled up. Puss followed, but came too late. "Well," says he, "it is no great matter; the bacon was rusty, and the mouse lean."

MORAL.—*Those who seek to cheat often find themselves outwitted.*

The Husbandman and the Stork

 HIN nets a farmer o er his furrows
spread,
And caught the cranes that on his
tillage fed.
And him a limping stork began
to pray,
Who fell with them into the
farmer's way:
"I am no crane: I don't consume
the grain:
That I'm a stork is from my colour plain;
A stork, than which no better bird doth live;
I to my father aid and succour give."
The man replied: "Good stork, I cannot tell
Your ways of life; but this I know full well:
I caught you with the spoilers of my seed;
With them, with whom I found you, you must bleed."

MORAL.—

*Walk with the bad, and hate will be as strong
'Gainst you as them, e'en though you no man wrong.*

"AND HIM A LIMPING STORK BEGAN TO PRAY"

𝕬 𝕱𝖔𝖝 𝖆𝖓𝖉 𝖆 𝕽𝖆𝖛𝖊𝖓

CERTAIN fox spied a raven upon a tree with a morsel in his beak. This set his mouth a-watering. But how to come at it was the question.

"Oh, thou blessed bird," says he, "the delight of gods, and of men!" and so he lays himself forth upon the gracefulness of the raven's person and the beauty of his plumes, his admirable gift of augury, and so forth. "And now," says the fox, "if thou hadst but a voice answerable to the rest of thy excellent qualities, the sun in the firmament could not show the world such another creature."

This flattery set the raven immediately opening his beak as wide as ever he could stretch, to give the fox a taste of his singing; but upon the opening of his mouth he drops his breakfast, which the fox at once snapped up, and then bade him remember that, whatever he had said of his beauty, he had spoken nothing yet of his brains.

MORAL.—*Extravagant flatterers may be suspected of wishing to gain something by their flattery.*

"BUT UPON THE OPENING OF HIS MOUTH HE DROPS HIS BREAKFAST"

The North Wind and the Sun

BETWIXT the North Wind and the
    Sun arose
A contest, which would soonest of
    his clothes
Strip a wayfaring clown, so runs
    the tale.
First Boreas blows an almost Thra-
    cian gale,
Thinking perforce to steal the man's
    capote.
He loos'd it not; but as the cold wind smote
More sharply, tighter round him drew the folds,
And sheltered by a crag his station holds.
And now the Sun at first peer'd gently forth,
And thaw'd the chills of the uncanny north.
Then in their turn his beams more amply plied,
Till sudden heat the clown's endurance tried:
Stripping himself, away his cloak he flung—
The Sun from Boreas thus a triumph wrung.

MORAL.—

The fable means: "My son, at mildness aim;
Persuasion more results than force may claim."

An Ant and a Pigeon

An ant dropped unluckily into the water as she was drinking at the side of a brook, so a wood pigeon, taking pity on her, threw her a little bough to catch hold of. The ant saved herself by this bough, and directly after spied a fellow with a gun, making a shot at the pigeon. Upon this discovery, she presently runs up to him and stings him. The fowler starts, and breaks his aim, and away flies the pigeon.

MORAL.—*A good service done may bring an unexpected reward.*

THE PROUD HORSE AND THE HUMBLE ASS

𝕬 𝕳𝖔𝖗𝖘𝖊 𝖆𝖓𝖉 𝖆𝖓 𝕬𝖘𝖘

In the days of old, when horses spoke Greek and Latin, and asses made syllogisms, there happened an encounter upon the road betwixt a proud pampered jade in the full course of his career, and a poor creeping ass under a heavy burden.

"Why, how now, sirrah," says the horse; "do you not see by these arms and trappings to what master I belong? And do you not understand that when I have that master of mine upon my back, the whole weight of the State rests upon my shoulders? Out of the way, thou slavish animal, or I'll tread thee to dirt!"

The wretched ass immediately slunk aside, with this envious reflection betwixt his teeth:

"What would I give to change conditions with that happy creature there!"

This fancy would not pass away, till it was his hap, some few days after, to see this very horse doing drudgery in a common cart.

"Why, how now, friend," says the ass; "how comes this about?"

"Only the chance of the war," says the other. "I was a soldier's horse, and my master carried me into a battle, where I was shot, hacked, and maimed; and you have here before your eyes the catastrophe of my fortune."

MORAL.—*Better to be free in a mean estate than subject to the sudden fluctuations of fortune.*

The Eagle, Cat, and Sow

There was an eagle, a cat, and a sow, that bred in a wood together. The eagle nested upon the top of a high oak, and the cat in the hollow trunk of it, while the sow lay at the bottom. The cat's heart was set upon mischief, and so she went with her tale to the eagle.

"Your Majesty had best look to yourself," says Puss, "for there is most certainly a plot upon you, and perchance upon poor me too; for yonder's a sow lying grubbing every day at the root of this tree. She'll bring it down at last, and then your little ones and mine are all at her mercy."

So soon as ever she had hammered a jealousy into the head of the eagle, away to the sow she goes, and tells her another story.

"Little do you think what a danger your litter is in! There's an eagle watching constantly up on this tree to make a prey of your piglings, and so soon as ever you are out of the way, she will certainly execute her design."

The cat upon this goes presently to her kittens again, keeping herself upon her guard all day, as if she were afraid, and steals out still at night to provide for her family. In one word, the eagle durst not stir for fear of the sow, and the sow durst not budge for fear of the eagle. So that they kept themselves upon their guard till they were starved, and left the care of their children to puss and her kittens.

MORAL.—*There can be no peace where talebearers are listened to.*

"SO SHE WENT WITH HER TALE TO THE EAGLE"

"IN PAIN HE TRIED TO CATCH IT"

An Ant and a Pigeon

The Eagle, Cat, and Sow

The Mouse and the Bull

A bull was bitten by a mouse. In
    pain
He tried to catch it; but 't was first
    to gain
The mouse-hole. With his horns, to
    raze its walls,
The bull essays, until asleep he falls,
Sinking, fatigued, hard by. Forth
    straightway hies
The peeping mouse, bites him again,
    and flies.
Uprose the bull, perplext what now
    to do,
And the mouse squeak'd to him
    this moral true:

"*Not always mighty are the great. 'T is seen
Sometimes, that stronger are the small and mean.*"

The Discontented Dog

A dog saw a cat on the top of a high wall, and said: "I wish I could get up there! It must be so nice to sit up so high! But I cannot climb."

And he was cross, and would not wag his tail. Then he came to a pond, and saw a fish in it. And he said: "I wish I could live in a pond all day! I should not then be so hot as I am now." And he would not look at the happy fish, but shut his eyes, and lay down on the grass.

By and by he heard the fish say: "Oh, I wish I could lie down on the fresh green grass like that dog! It does look so nice and warm out there!"

The dog sat up, and went back by the road he had come. As he went, he saw a bird flying in the air.

"I wish," said the bird, "I could play all day long, like that dog, and have a house made for me to live in. I have to make a nest, and my wings are so tired! Yet I must fly to and fro, day by day, till the work is done."

The dog went back to the high wall, and did not look at the cat.

But he heard her say: "There goes that spoilt old dog home to get his plate of meat. I wish I was as well off, and could get meat as he does. I have had no food all this hot day. I wish I was like that dog."

MORAL.—*It is foolish to envy others, forgetting our own advantages.*

A Fig Tree and a Thorn

A fig tree and a thorn were valuing themselves once upon the advantage that the one had over the other.

"Well," says the thorn, "what would you give for such flowers as these?"

"Very good," says the fig tree, "and what would you give for such fruit as this?"

"Well," says the other, "it would be against nature for a thorn to bring forth figs."

"Well," says the other again, "and it would be against nature too for a fig tree to bring forth flowers. Beside that, I have fruit, you see; that is much better."

MORAL.—*Boasting is not a virtue but a vanity.*

A Lion and a Mouse

Upon hearing the roaring of a beast in the wood, a mouse ran out to see what it was all about, and saw a lion hampered in a net. This accident brought to her mind how that she herself, but some few days before, had fallen under the paw of a certain generous lion, that let her go again. Upon enquiry, she found this to be that very lion, and so set herself presently to work upon the net— gnawed the threads to pieces—and in gratitude delivered her preserver.

MORAL.—*Little folks who have been kindly treated may be of great service to the powerful in their hour of need.*

"A MOUSE RAN OUT TO SEE WHAT IT WAS ALL ABOUT"

Boys and Frogs

A company of boys were watching frogs at the side of a pond, and as soon as any of them put up their heads, kept pelting them down again with stones.

"Children," says one of the frogs, "you never consider that though this may be play to you, 'tis death to us."

MORAL.—*Evil is wrought by want of thought as well as want of heart.*

"A COMPANY OF BOYS WERE WATCHING FROGS"

"FLYING OUT AT HIS OWN SHADOW"

256

𝔄 𝔖𝔨𝔦𝔱𝔱𝔦𝔰𝔥 𝔥𝔬𝔯𝔰𝔢

THERE goes a story of a restive, skittish jade, that had such a trick of rising, starting, and flying out at his own shadow, that he was not to be endured, for the discipline of the spur and the bit was wholly lost upon him. When his master found there was no reclaiming of him by the ordinary methods of horsemanship, he took him to task, saying:

"'Tis only a shadow that you boggle at, and what is that shadow but so much air that the light cannot come at? It has neither teeth nor claws, you see, nor anything else to hurt you. 'Twill neither break your shins nor block up your passage, and what are you afraid of then?"

"Well," says the horse, who it seems had more wit than his master, "'tis no new thing in the world even for the greatest heroes to shrink under the impression of panic terrors. What are all the sprites, ghosts, and goblins, that you yourselves tremble at, but phantoms and chimeras that are bred and shaped in your own brain?"

MORAL.—*Until we are better ourselves we should not blame others.*

𝕬 𝕮onsultation about 𝕾ecuring a 𝕮ity

THERE was a council of mechanics called to advise about the fortifying of a city. A bricklayer was for walling it with stone; a carpenter was of opinion that timber would be worth forty times as much; and after them up starts a currier. "Gentlemen," says he, "when you've said all that can be said, there's nothing in the world like leather."

MORAL.—*Each man thinks his own work of the chief importance in the world.*

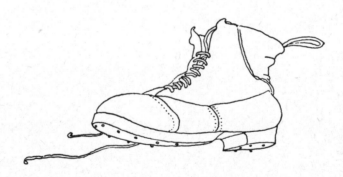

THE COUNCIL OF MECHANICS

259

"THE COLLATION WAS SERVED UP IN GLASSES WITH LONG NARROW NECKS"

𝔄 𝔉𝔬𝔵 𝔞𝔫𝔡 𝔞 𝔖𝔱𝔬𝔯𝔨

There was a great friendship once betwixt a fox and a stork, and the former would needs invite the other to a treat. They had several soups served up in broad dishes and plates, and so the fox fell to lapping himself, and bade his guest heartily welcome to what was before him. The stork found he was put upon, but set so good a face, however, upon his entertainment, that his friend by all means must take a supper with him that night in revenge. The fox made several excuses upon the matter of trouble and expense, but the stork would not be said Nay to, so that at last he promised him to come. The collation was served up in glasses with long narrow necks, and the best of everything that was to be had.

"Come," says the stork to his friend, "pray be as free as if you were at home," and so fell to very readily himself. The fox quickly found this to be a trick, though he could not but allow the justice of the revenge. For such a glass of sweetmeats to the one was just as much to the purpose as a plate of porridge to the other.

MORAL.—*Those who try tricks on others must expect to be made victims themselves.*

A Fox and a Sick Lion

CERTAIN lion, that pretended a fit of sickness, made it his observation, that of all the beasts in the forest, the fox never came near him; and so he wrote him word how ill he was, and how mighty glad he should be of his company, upon the score of ancient friendship and acquaintance. The fox returned the compliment with a thousand prayers for his recovery; but as for waiting upon him, he desired to be excused. "For," says he, "I find the traces of abundance of feet going to Your Majesty's palace, and not one that comes back again."

MORAL.—*The kindness of the ill-natured may well be suspected.*

The Kite, Hawk, and Pigeons

The pigeons, finding themselves persecuted by the kite, made choice of the hawk for their guardian. The hawk sets up for their protector, but, under countenance of their authority, makes more havoc in the dovehouse in two days than the kite could have done in twice as many months.

MORAL.—*It is no good trying to drive out one evil by a greater.*

Two Laden Asses

THERE'S an old story of two asses travelling upon the road, the one laden with oats, the other with money. The money merchant was so proud of his trust and of his bell that he went jerking and tossing his head, as if no ground would hold him. The other plodded on with his nose in the breech of his leader as gravely as one foot could follow another. While they are jogging on thus upon the way, out comes a band of highwaymen from the next wood, and falls upon the ass that carried the treasure. They beat, wound, and rifle him, and so leave him, without so much as taking the least notice of his fellow.

"Well," says the king's ass, "and for all this mischief I may e'en thank my money."

"Right!" says the other; "and it has been my happiness that I was not thought worth the robbing."

MORAL.—*The way of riches is a way beset by dangers.*

The Discontented Dog

A Lion and a Mouse

"OUT COMES A BAND OF HIGHWAYMEN"

"APPLIED A LIGHT, AND SENT IT FORTH"

The Man and the Fox

A man, that on his vines' and orchards' foe,
The fox, a strange affront design'd to throw,
Bandag'd its tail with tow, applied a light,
And sent it forth. Now Heaven's just oversight
Led the flame-bearer to its captor's fields.
It was the time for crops, when harvest yields
A hopeful prospect of abundant share.
The man pursued, deploring wasted care;
And Ceres did not bless his threshing-floor.

MORAL.—

One should be meek, and ne'er be vexed sore.
Anger a vengeance worth avoidance hath,
That bringeth damage to the quick-to-wrath.

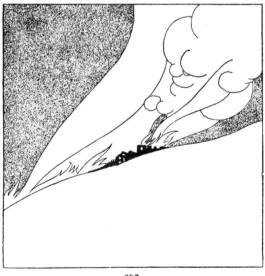

𝕿𝖍𝖊 𝕱𝖔𝖝 𝖙𝖍𝖆𝖙 𝕷𝖔𝖘𝖙 𝖍𝖎𝖘 𝕿𝖆𝖎𝖑

HERE was a fox that was caught in a trap, and was glad to save his life by leaving his tail behind him. It was so uncouth a sight for a fox to appear without a tail, that the very thought of it made him weary of his life, for it was a loss never to be repaired. But, however, for the better countenance of the scandal, he called a meeting of foxes at which he himself appeared and made a learned discourse upon the trouble, the uselessness, and the indecency of foxes wearing tails. He had no sooner had his say, than up rises another cunning fox, who desired to be informed, whether the worthy member that moved against the wearing of tails, gave his advice for the advantage of those that had tails, or to palliate the deformity and disgrace of those that had none.

MORAL.—*Interested advice needs careful examination.*

A Laden Ass and a Horse

As a horse and an ass were upon the way together, the ass cried out to his companion to ease him of his burden, though never so little; he should fall down dead else. The horse would not; and so his fellow servant sank under his load. His master, upon this, had the ass flayed, and laid his whole pack, skin and all, upon the horse.

"Well," says he, "this judgment is befallen me for my ill nature in refusing to help my brother in the depth of his distress."

MORAL.—*Unkindness to another brings sure punishment at some time.*

269

"A FIR TREE AND A BRAMBLE DISAGREED"

The Fir Tree and the Bramble

A FIR TREE and a bramble disagreed,
  For the fir always paid to self the
    meed
Of praise. " I 'm fine, well-grown in
    point of size,
And my straight top is neighbour to
    the skies.
'T is I am roof of mansions, keel of
    ships:
So much my comeliness all trees
    outstrips."
To whom the bramble said: " Keep
    well in view
The axe, whose business is thy trunk to hew,
And saws, that cut thee: haply thou 'lt prefer
To be the bramble, rather than the fir."

MORAL.—

All men of mark more rank and credit gain
Than meaner folks, but still more risks sustain.

"AND SEE IF I DON'T MAKE MYSELF NOW THE BIGGER OF THE TWO"

A Frog and an Ox

As a huge overgrown ox was grazing in a meadow, an old envious frog that stood gaping at him hard by called out to her little ones to take notice of the bulk of that monstrous beast; "and see," says she, "if I don't make myself now the bigger of the two." So she strained once, and twice, and went still swelling on and on, till in the end she burst.

MORAL.—*It is foolish to try to make ourselves appear greater than we are.*

An Old Lion

A lion, that in the days of his youth and strength had been very outrageous and cruel, came in the end to be reduced by old age and infirmity to the last degree of misery and contempt; insomuch that all the beasts of the forest — some out of insolence, others in revenge, some upon one pretence, some upon another—fell upon him by consent. He was a miserable creature to all intents and purposes; but nothing went so near the heart of him in his distress, as to find himself battered by the heel of an ass.

MORAL.—*Those who behave as tyrants in their strength must expect to be treated with contempt in their weakness.*

274

"HE WAS A MISERABLE CREATURE TO ALL INTENTS AND PURPOSES"

𝕬 𝖂𝖔𝖒𝖆𝖓 𝖆𝖓𝖉 𝖍𝖊𝖗 𝕳𝖊𝖓

A good country woman having a hen that every day laid for her a nice large egg, fancied that if she gave it yet more corn the hen might be made to lay twice a day. So she gave the bird more and more food until it grew so fat that it quite gave up laying eggs at all.

MORAL.—*It is good to let well alone.*

"SO SHE GAVE THE BIRD MORE AND MORE FOOD"

"AN OLD MAN AND A LITTLE BOY WERE DRIVING AN ASS"
278

An Old Man and an Ass

An old man and a little boy were driving an ass before them to the next market to sell.

"Why, have you no more wit," says one to the man upon the way, "that you and your son trudge it afoot, and let the ass go light?" So the man set the boy upon the ass, and footed it himself.

"Why, sirrah," says another after this, to the boy, "you lazy rogue you, must you ride, and let your ancient father go afoot?" The man upon this took down his boy, and got up himself.

"Do you see," says a third, "how the lazy old knave rides himself, and the poor little child has much ado to creep after him!" The father, upon this, took up his son behind him. The next they met asked the old man whether his ass were his own or no. He said: "Yes."

"Troth, there's little sign of it," says the other, "by your loading him thus."

"Well," says the fellow to himself, "what am I to do now? For I am laughed at if either the ass be empty, or if one of us rides, or both," and so in the conclusion he bound the ass's legs together with a cord, and they tried to carry him to market with a pole upon their shoulders betwixt them. This was such sport to everybody who saw it that the old fellow in great wrath threw down the ass into a river, and so went his way home again. The good man, in fine, was willing to please everybody, but had the ill fortune to please nobody, and lost his ass into the bargain.

MORAL.—*It is foolish trying to please everybody.*

𝔄 𝕮𝕚𝕥𝕪 𝕸𝕠𝕦𝕤𝕖 𝕒𝕟𝕕 𝕒 𝕮𝕠𝕦𝕟𝕥𝕣𝕪 𝕸𝕠𝕦𝕤𝕖

There goes an old story of a country mouse that invited a city sister of hers to a country collation, where she spared for nothing that the place afforded, putting before her crusts and cheese-parings, oatmeal and bacon, and the like. Now the city dame was so well-bred as seemingly to take all in good part, but yet at last—

"Sister," says she, after the civilest fashion, "why will you be miserable when you may be happy? Why will you lie pining and pinching yourself in such a lonesome starving course of life as this, when 'tis but going to town along with me to enjoy all the pleasures and plenty that your heart can wish?"

This was a temptation the country mouse was not able to resist; so that away they trudged together, and about midnight got to their journey's end. The city mouse showed her friend the larder, the pantry, the kitchen, and other offices where she laid her stores; and after this carried her into the parlour, where they found, yet upon the table, the relics of a mighty entertainment of that very night. The city mouse carved her companion of what she liked best, and so to it they fell upon a velvet couch together. The poor bumpkin that had never seen nor heard of such doings before blessed herself at the change of her condition, when (as ill luck would have it) all on a sudden the doors flew open, and in comes many people with their dogs, and put the poor mice to their wits' end how to save their skins. The stranger made a shift for the present to

A City Mouse and a Country Mouse

The Dog in a Manger

slink into a corner, where she lay trembling and panting till the company went their way. So soon as ever the house was quiet again—

"Well, my Court sister," says she, "if this be the way of your town gambols, I'll e'en back to my cottage and my mouldy cheese again; for I had much rather nibble crusts without fear or danger in my own hole, than be mistress of the whole world with perpetual cares and alarms."

MORAL.—*Better is it to have plain fare and peace than luxury and many dangers.*

The Dog in a Manger

A churlish, envious cur was gotten into a manger, and there lay growling and snarling so as to keep the horses from their provender. The dog could eat none of it himself, and yet rather ventured the starving of his own carcass than he would suffer anything else to be the better for it.

MORAL.—*To prevent others using what we cannot use ourselves is currish.*

282

"A CHURLISH, ENVIOUS CUR WAS GOTTEN INTO A MANGER"

283

MERCURY AND THE SCULPTOR
284

𝕸𝖊𝖗𝖈𝖚𝖗𝖞 𝖆𝖓𝖉 𝖆 𝕾𝖈𝖚𝖑𝖕𝖙𝖔𝖗

ERCURY had a desire once to learn what credit he had in the world, and he knew no better way than to put on the shape of a man, and take occasion to discuss the matter with a sculptor. So away he went to the house of a great master, where among other curious figures he saw several excellent statues of the gods. The first of which he asked the price was a Jupiter.

"Well," says Mercury, "and what's the price of that Juno there?"

The carver set that a little higher. The next figure was a Mercury, with his rod and his wings, and all the ensigns of his commission.

"Why, this is as it should be," says he to himself, "for here am I in the quality of Jupiter's messenger, and the patron of artisans, with all my trade about me. And now will this fellow ask me fifteen times as much for this as he did for the other," and so he put it to him, what he valued that piece at.

"Why, truly," says the sculptor, "you seem to be a civil gentleman; give me but my price for the other two, and you shall e'en have that into the bargain."

MORAL.—*Those who set too high a value upon themselves are often but little valued by others.*

THE FLY AND THE ANT
286

The Fly and the Ant

A fly said thus to an ant, whom she met in the summer:
"Thou art for certain a poor and despicable beast, who,
though thou hast wings to fly on high, yet, like a mean-
spirited wretch, creepest always on the earth, and labourest
hard to get a sordid livelihood, eating only a little corn, and
drinking only a little water. I, on the contrary, soar aloft,
and without any labour take my place at the most costly
feasts, where I feed on the most delicious morsels, and drink
from gold and silver vessels the most exquisite liquors. I
sleep in purple beds, and there kiss the ruddy cheeks of the
most beautiful women."

To which the ant answered:
"Full dearly thou payest for all the delights which
thou enjoyest, by living, as thou dost, in continual dread of
being crushed to pieces by fans and fly-flaps, of being
caught by clammy sweets, or drowned in feastful bowls.
But say the best that can befall thee, thy short-lived days
and pleasures soon will end, when the first winter comes
thou certainly must die, and leave for ever these mistaken
joys. These are the thoughts that convince me how much
my happiness surpasses thine, and that make me and the
dear companions of my labours employ ourselves with great
satisfaction and content in hoarding up in the summer a
sufficient quantity of food to support us in quiet and security
all the winter."

MORAL.—*Thrift and industry lead to settled happiness denied
to idleness and luxury.*

𝔗𝔥𝔢 𝔆𝔥𝔢𝔢𝔰𝔢

Two cats had, by some means or other, got a cheese between them, to which they had undoubtedly an equal right. Disputes (as they often happen on ill-gotten goods) arose between them how to make an equal division, and to end the controversy they agreed Dame Justice should decide it.

Well, away these contenders go to a monkey, a neighbour of theirs, who was chief clerk to a judge that lived in the village, and whom one would take for my lord himself, especially when he had his furs and cornered cap on.

The cheese was brought into court before my Lord Pug, who, sitting on the bench with a very serious and demure countenance (you must think), coughed, put his thumbs into his girdle, and commanded silence.

This done, he very gravely divides it into two parts, and, holding up the scales with one hand, puts in the two pieces with the other.

"We sit here to do justice," says he, "and therefore let us weigh this matter with circumspection. 'Let equity always prevail', say I. So; but—a—this piece here outweighs the other a little, methinks," and bites off a large bit.

"On my conscience," says he, "I believe now this will do." But it happened the other piece drew down the scale. "So, so," says he; "now this piece is the heavier. But I'll make both equal by and by, as you shall see, for I love to do the thing that is right," and bites off another piece for the same weighty reason.

"'WE SIT HERE TO DO JUSTICE,' SAYS HE"

When he had made a third trial, one scale only just drew down the other.

"'Tis mighty well, my lord, now," said the cats; "pray give it us, we are very well satisfied."

"Satisfied! why aye, you may be so, indeed," quoth the monkey; "but if you are satisfied, Justice is not. You are a couple of ignorant fellows; why, how can you imagine that we will let things be decided after such a gross manner as you would have it. No, no, this is a nice point, and we may perhaps direct a special verdict," and began gently to nibble away from the larger piece what he thought it might exceed the other in, and thus by strict rules of Justice he had pretty well devoured good part of both pieces.

The two antagonists, seeing this, desired, however, that they might have the rest for their share.

"Soft and fair, good gentlemen," says the monkey; "you may retire if you please, for what remains belongs to me for my fees; for we must do justice to ourselves as well as other people. So you may go about your business, and be thankful it is no worse."

MORAL:—*A knave can always find an excuse for his knavery.*

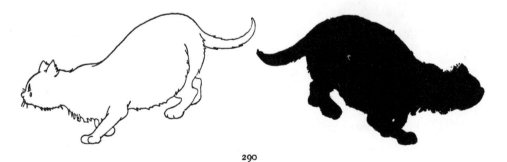

𝔄gainst the 𝔥ard to 𝔖uit

WERE I a pet of fair Calliope,
    I would devote the gifts conferr'd
        on me
    To dress in verse old Æsop's lies
        divine;
    For verse, and they, and truth, do
        well combine;
    But, not a favourite on the Muses'
        hill,
    I dare not arrogate the magic
        skill,
To ornament these charming stories.
A bard might brighten up their glories,
No doubt. I try—what one more wise must do.
Thus much I have accomplish'd hitherto:—
    By help of my translation,
    The beasts hold conversation,
In French, as ne'er they did before,
Indeed, to claim a little more,
The plants and trees, with smiling features,
Are turn'd by me to talking creatures.
Who says, that this is not enchanting?
"Ah," say the critics, "hear what vaunting!
From one whose work, all told, no more is
Than half a dozen baby stories."
Would you a theme more credible, my censors,
In graver tone, and style which now and then soars?

Then list! For ten long years the men of Troy,
By means that only heroes can employ,
Had held the allied hosts of Greece at bay—
Their minings, batterings, stormings day by day,
Their hundred battles on the crimson plain,
Their blood of thousand heroes, all in vain—
When, by Minerva's art, a horse of wood,
Of lofty size, before their city stood,
Whose flanks immense the sage Ulysses hold,
Brave Diomed, and Ajax fierce and bold,
Whom, with their myrmidons, the huge machine
Would bear within the fated town unseen,
To wreak upon its very gods their rage—
Unheard-of stratagem, in any age,
Which well its crafty authors did repay. . . .
   " Enough, enough," our critic folks will say;
     " Your period excites alarm,
   Lest you should do your lungs some harm;
     And then your monstrous wooden horse,
       With squadrons in it at their ease,
        Is even harder to endorse
   Than Reynard cheating Raven of his cheese.
       And, more than that, it fits you ill
        To wield the old heroic quill."
Well, then, a humbler tone, if such your will is:—
Long sigh'd and pined the jealous Amaryllis
For her Alcippus, in the sad belief,
None, save her sheep and dog, would know her grief.
Thyrsis, who knows, among the willow slips,
And hears the gentle shepherdess's lips
   Beseech the kind and gentle zephyr

To bear these accents to her lover. . . .
    "Stop!" says my censor:
    "To laws of rhyme quite irreducible,
That couplet needs again the crucible;
      Poetic men, sir,
     Must nicely shun the shocks
     Of rhymes unorthodox."
A curse on critics! hold your tongue!
Know I now how to end my song?
Of time and strength what greater waste
Than my attempt to suit your taste?

MORAL.—

Some men, more nice than wise,
There's naught that satisfies.

The End